To my father who gave me
my love of mountains

STEVE BERRY

Straight Up

Himalayan Kingdoms Ltd.
www.mountainkingdoms.com

Straight Up
by Steve Berry

First published in 2012 by Himalayan Kingdoms Ltd.

Copyright © Steve Berry 2012

Himalayan Kingdoms Ltd.
20 Long Street, Wotton-under-Edge, Gloucestershire GL12 7BT, United Kingdom

Steve Berry has asserted his rights under the Copyright, Designs and Patents Act 1988
to be identified as author of this work.

Photography by the author unless otherwise credited.

This book is a work of non-fiction based on the life, experiences and recollections of
Steve Berry. In some limited cases the names of people, places, dates and sequences
or the detail of events have been changed solely to protect the privacy of others.
The author has stated to the publishers that, except in such minor respects not
affecting the substantial accuracy of the work, the contents of the book are true.

A CIP catalogue record for this book is available from the British Library.

ISBN 978-1-906148-47-8

10 9 8 7 6 5 4 3 2 1

Every effort has been made to obtain the necessary permissions with reference to copyright
material, both illustrative and quoted. We apologise for any omissions in this respect and
will be pleased to make the appropriate acknowledgements in any future edition.

Designed and typeset in Garamond by Jane Beagley, Vertebrate Graphics Ltd.
www.v-graphics.co.uk

Printed and bound in China by Latitude Press

CONTENTS

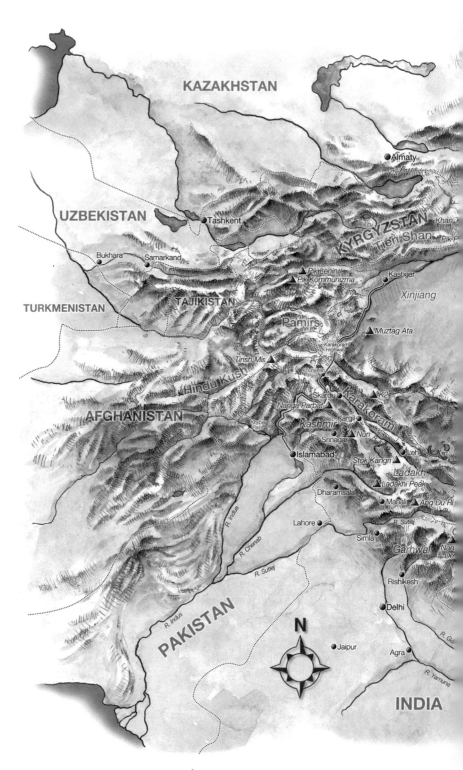

Map of the Himalaya

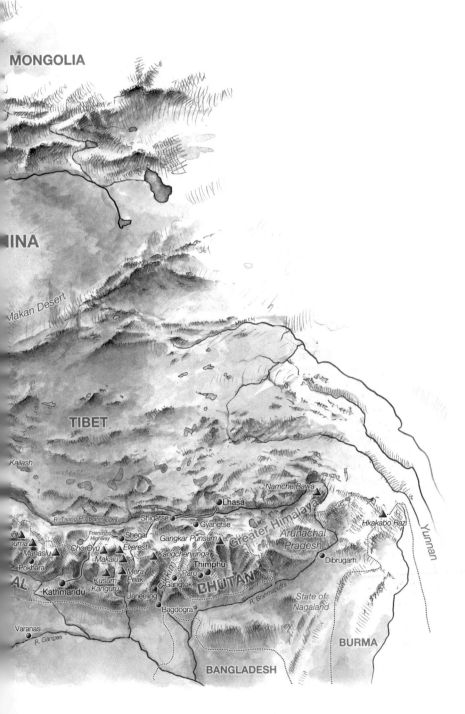

MONGOLIA

IINA

Makan Desert

TIBET

Kailash

Namche Bawa

R. Tsang Po (Brahmaputra)

Shigatse

Lhasa

Gyangtse

Greater Himalaya

Hkakabo Razi

Friendship
Highway

Shegar

Gangkar Punsum

Arunachal
Pradesh

Yunnan

urma

Manaslu

Cho Oyu

Everest

Kangchenjunga

Dibrugarh

Pokhara

Makalu

Mera
Peak

Thimphu

Kusum
Kanguru

Paro

Gangtok

BHUTAN

AL

Kathmandu

Darjeeling

R. Brahmaputra

State of
Nagaland

Bagdogra

Varanasi

R. Ganges

BURMA

BANGLADESH

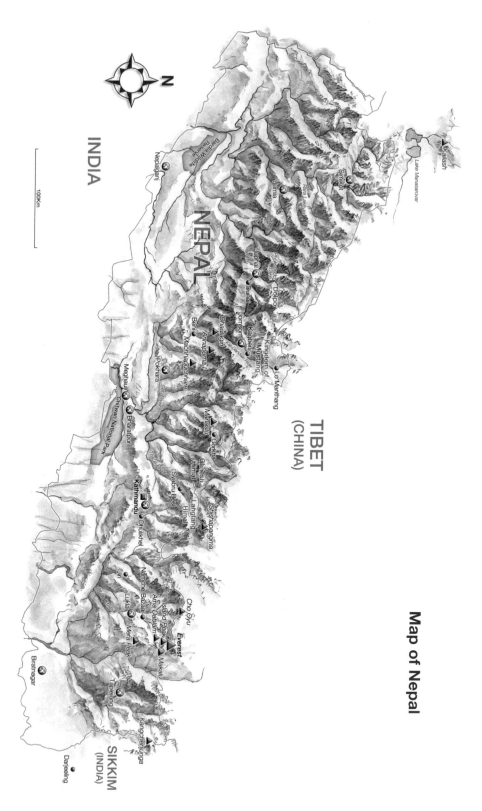

Map of Nepal

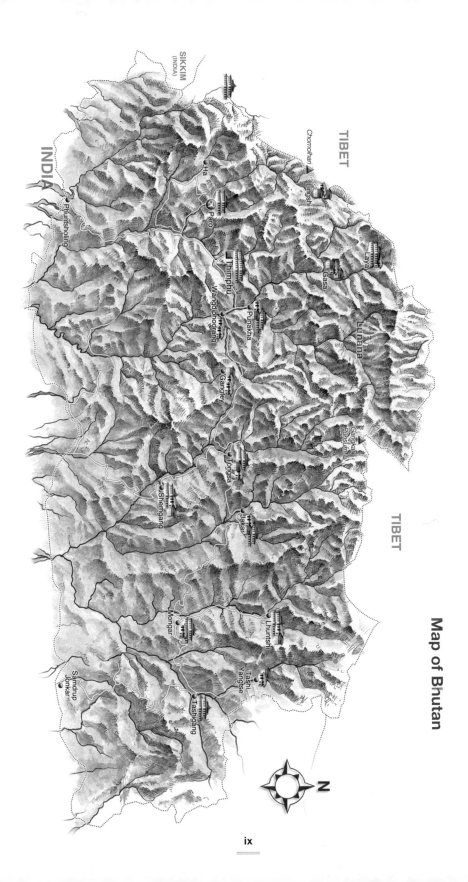

Map of Bhutan

FOREWORD

I HAVE KNOWN STEVE BERRY now for 12 years. My first meeting with Steve was at Bristol when he invited me to do a lecture for the Wilderness Lectures programme. After the show I stayed at Steve's house and received such warm hospitality, just like we offer here at our Sherpa home. I felt like I had known Steve for a long time even though I had only just met him. It was a great moment for me meeting Steve and hearing all about his adventures of climbing in the Himalaya, and meeting his lovely family.

Steve is a mountaineer who has climbed peaks in the Himalaya from India and Bhutan to Nepal. He was the first British climber to ascend Mount Nun in 1981, the highest mountain in Northern India, in the state of Jammu and Kashmir.

The Himalaya have a way of entrancing those who enter their orbit; to create a spiritual adventure and fond memories that last for a lifetime. This is not merely because they are the highest mountains in the world, but also because of the dimensions of spirituality and the special grace of force that the Himalayan peaks have to offer.

Steve, who has been trekking and climbing in the Himalaya many decades, admirably captures the joy and the beauty of the mountains in this book. He explains his chapters from a different vantage point and with great feeling. He gives a very honest account of his journeys that have taken him from Mount Nun and his father's expedition, to the Turquoise Mountain Cho Oyu. His love for the Bhutan Mountains and its people are so special in his life.

As I read this book and looked at the images, I was reminded of my own journeys and climbs in my beloved Himalaya and Antarctica. It's a great pleasure to see these mountains and the people who live under the shadows of the Himalaya being brought to a large number of people through the pages of Steve's book. It is only through knowing of the beautiful places of our world that people like Steve get inspired to live in that world more responsibly and caringly, preserving such grandeur and beauty for generations to come.

I congratulate Steve for his wonderful stories that he has expressed with true honesty, purely for the love of the Himalaya and its people, whom he has admired and made wonderful friends amongst, and continues to do so. I am sure this book will be a source of positive inspiration for many readers.

Tashi Tenzing
Grandson of Sherpa Tenzing Norgay and three times Everest summiteer

INTRODUCTION

ON THE FACE OF IT the real world seems so ordinary, normal, simple even. There are the trees and their leaves, grass, plants and animals, insects, the earth itself, clouds and rain, stone and sky. So it would seem with the lives we have; we eat, we defecate, we sleep, we breathe, we move, we reproduce. Why should there be anything fantastical beyond this natural world? Why shouldn't mankind have stuck with hunting, growing things and protecting himself from his neighbours? After all that's what all the other creatures do. On the face of it everything's so normal. It should be normal, but then again it's not. Reality in fact is not the slightest bit normal. The universe stretches to infinity in every direction, crowded with an infinite number of galaxies each containing such vast numbers of stars and solar systems that our stretched minds find it hard to cope. In the other direction our scientists tell us that everything is made of invisibly small spinning objects whose vast numbers are even more difficult to comprehend. Abnoreality is a very big thing indeed.

Well, even if reality is composed of an incomprehensible collection of scattered matter, *that* could be soaked up by sanity, provided it all followed a set of logical rules, but there do appear to be some pretty strange things going on behind the scenes. Life has designed some staggeringly clever things which for my money cannot just be passed off by theories of natural selection. At an atomic level DNA shows an intelligent manipulation of matter. This process of eggs and sperm coming together in a variety of inventive ways; that's not just luck, and sorry, but I don't believe that a billion creatures flung themselves off cliffs flapping their appendages until one day two of them rose into the air and started breeding as seagulls. Behind a front of normality, which we grow up to so readily accept, there are stranger forces at work.

Not just in the matter of creation, or the creation of matter, but in how the past, present and future are connected, how we as people are joined in inexplicably odd ways, how fate has a hand in normality, how every now and then there are solid markers to tell us we are going in the right direction, or not, as the case may be. How occasionally there are outrageous experiences which occur to dumbfound our conditioned selves. Telepathy, astral travel, levitation, communication with the after-life, faith healing, visions of the future to name but one or two talents our motley race chances on from time to time. Even through our 'science' we have almost inadvertently discovered we can speak to each other by the use of fashionable handsets, freeze time on celluloid, send moving pictures at the speed of light, look in detail at the insides of our bodies, and catapult metal objects to the far reaches of our solar system and beyond.

So why should we expect things to be 'normal', they patently are not, and we have every right to expect extraordinary forces to be working on a plan for our lives. Had I been asking these questions in Mediaeval times I no doubt would have believed God had the answers. Now all I see is a host of arrogant religions claiming ownership of the patents to the infinite, and fighting each other for the right to exist. A whiff of the absolute no doubt touches the mental nostrils of every culture but the existence of one God to rule them all; I doubt it. All the religions have got it wrong and mankind will continue his search for appropriate questions to discover the ultimate truths of the universe. All the tools we have in our individual search for perfection are the subtle power of words, and emotions to set them free. Will exemplary characters emerge wielding words to provide the all powerful answers in the end? Possibly. In any case forget normality; we are now a far cry from the simple, normal life of breeding and farming.

And it seems to me that humankind is never happier than when things are not normal. We spend most of our time in a world of fantasy of one sort or another. We devour anything that is fiction, and chase the ends of imaginary rainbows in the hope of finding a pot of gold that will convey us into some consumer paradise. In our ordinary lives we dream of impossible sexual situations, success that would elevate us to a point of veneration, and personal acts of bravery or charity that would automatically earn us the respect we imagine we deserve. Our television is ninety percent fantasy ten percent poorly presented fact, the biggest blockbuster films are of magical heroes quashing quadruped aliens or vanquishing evil wizards. Barely a moment goes by when we are not absorbed by either our personal fantasies or the fantastical world of others. Even in our sleep when you would think that everyday normality would prevail, we experience detailed phantasmagorical worlds of the bizarre that our waking selves would be incapable of inventing. Not content with the birds and the bees we are continuously tampering with reality, poking it, prodding it, whipping up its potential in the hope we can slow the decay of our houses of flesh, or create the perfect being. The fact is that reality is boring if taken on face value, and mankind slavers for excitement. Mankind feeds on fantasy. We are utterly obsessed by it and our spirits crave more and more.

I think fantasy hits its peak when we are young, especially when hormones and adrenalin have right of way in our veins. The young have blind confidence in their abilities and a sense of indestructibility and close their eyes to the obvious, that big mountains are very dangerous places.

So it was for me, and it was not until long after I started to fulfil my own fantasies of exploring the Himalaya that I was to discover that there especially, not everything is what it seems.

My first climbing memory is of a gnarled old oak tree that grew on the village green right opposite the manor house that we had rented as a family in Kirtlington, Oxfordshire. The village lads would often climb up and into the tree which was so old it was hollow inside. Dad drove some six inch nails into the trunk to help me get up. I must have been only four at the time. The second climbing memory is not so happy. We had moved to the nearby village of Chesterton and this time had rented the servants' quarters of an old deserted mansion. One day, aged seven, I tied my younger brother on one end of mum's washing line and we climbed into yew trees behind the house. As we moved along some

Kirtlington Manor.   *Photo: Berry Family Collection*

branches my brother fell down one side of the branch we were on, and I fell down the other. We were left dangling and screaming for help. Luckily our father heard us and rushed out of the house and cut us down before we died of asphyxiation. We received a sound thrashing with the leather end of a horsewhip. It didn't put us off though.

We were a solid middle class family with a few skeletons in the closet like everyone else. After all we do live in the real world and nothing is perfect. Dad was a self-made man, who had risen from his illegitimate beginnings from mining stock in Yorkshire to become a Major in the British Army in India during the Second World War, and afterwards to become a chartered surveyor and pillar of the community. He had climbed in the Indian Himalaya during times of leave, and from an early age I remember there were always stories of India, and when he was de-mobbed from the army, many pieces of our furniture had been sent back from Bombay with his kit.

I admired his achievements but hated his Victorian views, his strict discipline and the rather narrow minded, black and white view he had of the world; it led to too much prejudice in my view. He was clever and could be utterly charming, but if you got on the wrong side of him like as not you would find yourself bettered in a court of law with damages and costs to meet. Despite the fact he had lived in India dad also suffered from the typical type of barely concealed colonial racial prejudice that was widespread with his generation. He also held a very low opinion of the mental abilities of Americans. He cared deeply about

LEFT Maj. Roy Berry.   RIGHT My mother, myself and my brother. *Photos: Berry Family Collection*

many other things and I have so far painted much too black a picture of him. He built flats for the elderly, rescued buildings he thought had architectural merit from being bulldozed, and sat on the Town Council. He absolutely loved our mother who in fairness had been sent from heaven to look after us. She came from a one time wealthy family who had made their money from a fleet of trawlers which operated out of Grimsby and Fleetwood. The fleet had not been modernised and the money was fast dissipating, but still they lived a rather grand style of life, and granny played canasta once a week and all her friends wore furs. Grandpa Olliff had been gassed three times in the First World War and never really worked again afterwards, but I digress.

Dad certainly loved the mountains most of all. Weeks away in North Wales were the only time we got on well together. We ticked off all the peaks over two thousand feet listed in a book by W. A. Poucher, always finishing with an ascent of Snowdon. We stayed at Mrs. William's farmhouse which had no electricity and a toilet built over a stream, and I remember after one long day walking in the hills dad drinking twenty seven cups of tea from Mrs. William's bone china tea cups.

When we were living at Kirtlington, and I must still have only been five, dad came home after a climbing trip to North Wales, and taking off his shirt revealed that he was black and blue all over. He had fallen off trying to lead *Munich Climb* on Tryfan and with the rope only having been tied round his waist had sustained a lot of bruising. He stopped climbing after that until I was seventeen when mum let him take me on my first proper rock climb, on the proviso that we employed a professional guide. Ron James took us up *The Parson's Nose* on Crib y Ddysgl and from that day on I couldn't wait to do more. The following day in fact dad and his best friend Dr. Plint both failed to lead *Pulpit Route* on Tryfan and I pleaded to have a go. Successfully reaching the belay after a steep little wall I was as high as a kite, and thereafter gave up tennis, cricket and athletics and spent any spare time climbing.

One of the main reasons for me moving to Bristol aged twenty one was because I knew I would have the Avon Gorge on my doorstep. It didn't take long to make friends with the bunch of young climbers who were always hanging around Stan's tea van in the car park below the main area of limestone cliffs. Some became friends for life, but later quite a few died in the mountains. We were wild and free, couldn't care less about authority, drove our cars far too fast, smashed them up too often, partied, smoked cannabis, ate magic mushrooms, and competed with each other for the physical affections of the dismally small number of females who were attracted by our company. We spent all our spare time rock-climbing and discussing individual moves in great detail in the pub afterwards.

Life went on like this for a good many years. Some of our number became world class rock-climbers in their own right, and before convention and matrimony infiltrated the group, we gave free rein to ambition. We thrashed an assortment of old bangers across France to the Alps, we climbed above topless beaches near St. Tropez, and we played with our American cousins at the Mecca that all rock-climbers aspire to, Yosemite, California. Eventually, of course, we began to fantasise about the Himalaya and this book is a collection of some of those adventures.

I have tried to tell the truth as far as I can. I mean why the hell not; the truth is the truth after all, and I have never pretended to be a starched white shirt. I have, however, not revealed certain rumours which might hurt living relatives of friends who have died in the big hills, or which would spoil my own relations with certain foreign governments.

CHAPTER 1

The Very First Time

THE BEAR HAD GONE THROUGH the only patch of snow where we could pitch a tent just a few hours before. We knew this for certain as it had snowed in the morning as Matt and I had laboured three thousand feet, with crucifying loads, from our last camp in the Solang Nala valley in the Indian state of Himachal Pradesh. The bear prints were still crisp.

Before we set off Matt had given me a convincing impression of knowing where he was going, so I followed him out of the dripping, soggy forest, up through the snow line and over the glacial moraine. Descending a thousand feet we had found a level place for our tent, but the fresh snow was criss-crossed by bear tracks. We had no choice – we had had to camp there. It was the only place, and it would soon be dark. The bear's imprint was almost as big as my mountaineering boot and you could clearly see the sharp claw marks. We were already

Base Camp, Ladakhi Peak. Bear tracks behind camp.

1

two thousand feet above the snow line and were amazed to see the tracks leading off and up several thousand feet more above us. We concluded that it must have come this way heading north to cross the Tentu Pass, 16,000ft, which gives access into another valley system to the west.

Another thing that amazed us was that, after examining the tracks, it was clear that the bear walked for long distances upright. Evenly spaced prints, not two on the right followed by two on the left. We knew nothing about bears – did they walk long distances upright? Could it perhaps be a Yeti? The paw shape and the claw marks were perfectly visible. It had to be a bear.

Fresh bear tracks.

We pitched our two-man tent on a stamped-out snow platform, cooked a frugal supper, and organised our climbing gear for the morning. Excitement, adrenalin and fear fought for space in our young heads. There we were, hoping to climb an 18,000ft/5,500 metre mountain, days from the nearest village, camped on the snow on the only level spot for miles, surrounded by bear tracks that could only have been made a few hours previously. We were trespassers, and not far away was an irresistibly powerful and savage animal with big teeth and sharp claws. Finally, we rationed ourselves to a few slugs from our small plastic bottle of whisky before making our preparations in case the bear came back. We wrapped the heads of our two ice axes with handkerchiefs, soaked them with some of our precious petrol, and propped them in the awning with matches nearby. We were laughing a lot by now.

This was India and we were just two young, fairly impoverished men far from home. We had only been able to afford the services of two porters, who carried our kit up to the end of the valley, and had then departed. We also knew for a fact that there were bears in the area as we had already had one encounter. At the end of the first day I had gone for a walk on my own above camp and seen two in a meadow about a quarter of a mile away. I had backed down the hill carefully without them spotting me. The local people in the town of Manali had told us several frightening stories about the 'Lal Balu', or red bear. Of how a local woman had been abducted by a male bear and had lived as its wife for several years before escaping. Of how people who had gone for a walk in the woods on their own had never been seen again – eaten by the bears it was said. To be honest we had counted on them not being above the snowline.

It was my father's influence that had brought me to India. He had served there in the war and during his leave had ventured into the Himalaya. My brother and I grew up with stories of his adventures in those privileged days of the Raj when a young British officer could wangle the use of army trucks, lay his hands on expedition kit, and be entertained in grand style by local dignitaries. As children we had rummaged through tea trunks in our loft and pulled out his old expedition gear, pretending to be brave explorers. In his rather obsessive way there were excessively annotated maps, expedition reports, photo albums of his climbs and copies of the Himalayan Club Journal, with more copious notes in the margin. The romance had rubbed off on me, and from a very early age I had made a solemn promise to myself that one day I too would go exploring in the greatest mountain range on earth.

For a long time normal life interfered with this ambition. I had to study, find a job, buy a house, but with no wife in prospect at the age of twenty eight, and with rents to cover my mortgage, I decided it was now or never. Unfortunately my friends in the Bristol rock-climbing circle were all out of funds, or tied down, except one – my regular climbing partner, Matt Peacock. Although his appearance was utterly conventional Matt led a very different life to most. He had rebelled against his father's desire that he become a bank manager, and instead had followed a life of working night shifts in a bakery, six months at a stretch, and having saved enough he would then travel alone throughout India. Six months work, six months travel in India – that's how he had been living for some years now. He would be my Indian guru; he knew stuff that would see us out of tight corners. He knew all the scams conmen would try to pull on us, and his knowledge of backstreets and bazaars, the workings of Indian road and rail, and how to bargain with rickshaw drivers was an added bonus. Besides which I knew that in Matt's company I would live high on laughter. Behind National Health glasses was a mystic, a madman, a prankster and a very talented climber.

Anyway Matt had persuaded me that he knew a couple of 'easy' peaks just north of Manali, that shambolic Indian hill station popular

The enigmatic Matt Peacock.

with hippies, which is surrounded by forests, terraced hillsides and pretty villages, and a stone's throw from the mountains of my father's black and white photographs. That place I had so long wanted to reach. I had handed in my notice to Hartnell Taylor and Cook, a fine upstanding firm of surveyors, purchased a ticket on Iraqi Air from a decidedly shady bucket shop, and told my tenants I would be back, God willing, in three months. I had made a will which stated that in the event of my untimely demise, my friends would have to perform a variety of outrageous tasks to get a share of my meagre estate. I had said fond farewells to my despairing and worried parents, and arranged to meet Matt in Delhi. He was as usual mid way through another huge tour of his beloved India.

Iraqi Air had taken off, landed with a technical fault, taken off again and not worsened the airline's safety record by making it all the way to Delhi, via Baghdad where the airport was being repaired after a bomb blast. I disembarked with an Indian gentleman who was smuggling in watches by wearing scores of them under his clothes, on both arms and legs. This was 1977 long before metal detectors had become the bain of air travel. Leaving the Jumbo the heat hit me with the force akin to opening an oven door. India is a shock from the word go.

Here is how it was – we had very little money between us and so every rupee seemed important. We argued with the rickshaw boys until sometimes they would drive off in disgust, we stayed in hotels where rats ran across the end of the room, we got bitten by bed bugs, and we ate our food from street vendors. Matt was an old India hand and well-acclimatised, but within forty eight hours I was curled up in a foetal position wishing I had not been tempted by the sweet cakes in the market. However, the train tickets to Chandigarh were already bought and Matt shepherded me through the heat and the crowds and onto a steam train heading north. I literally rolled off the train at Chandigarh where an old Indian gentleman befriended us and guided us to the First Class Waiting Room, while he found us a taxi and took us to a hotel. Soon I was tucked up in bed feeling like death. I lay there for two days, in between all too frequent visits to the bathroom, and our old Indian friend came in each day bringing us bananas. We found he could quote from memory huge chunks of Shakespeare. While serving in the Indian Army he had joined the Drama Society and had acted in King Lear. Having studied the play at school I knew his renditions were word perfect. Finally, having expertly made us his friend for life he made his pitch for a handout. How could we refuse. From the sweltering plains we had then travelled twelve hours through the foothills on a public bus to Manali. There had been punctures and landslides on the way, but the most serious equipment failure of the battered, vomit-covered bus was the silencing of the Italian triple air horns. As these were in constant use it was rather important that they were fixed!

Arrive in Manali we eventually did and, after one flea bitten hotel, we shifted to the local Youth Hostel, next to a small shanty town of Tibetan refugees, whose dogs frequently harassed us. There we settled for eleven days and, in between bouts of bad weather and illness, we prepared our lazy bodies for our first high altitude climb of an 18,000 ft mountain called Ladakhi Peak, by suitably punishing day walks in the foothills. Finally though we had to tear ourselves away from the flesh pots, and having hired two porters to help carry to the snowline, set off on our first Himalayan climb.

The night was dark, extremely dark, and not a breath of wind even rustled the tent. Altitude, whisky and childish humour had meant we had laughed ourselves to a standstill. We had used our two favourite camp games. The first was taking it in turns to invent more and more ridiculous ways of crossing the Sahara desert, while the other was to describe in as much detail as possible our own favourite food dishes. When you are starving on a diet of rehydrated food and powdered

Relatively vomit free bus with a puncture.

mash, and have been away from home for some weeks, this is an intensely painful, but hilariously funny experience. The object of the game is to find a simple English dish, such as treacle tart covered in double Cornish cream, which will reduce your partner to a writhing heap, begging for mercy. We had finished the whisky and had all but drifted off to sleep when suddenly the tent shook uncontrollably. I remember lying as still as possible, but at the same time fumbling in quiet desperation trying to find the matches, expecting a painful, ignominious death at any second. The joke was on us, however, for all it was was a freak but powerful wind blasting down the mountainside without warning.

We were up next day at 4.00 a.m. climbing in earnest now, cramponing up the frozen snow slopes, our tent receding to a small dot below us. The incredibly steep and fierce peak of Hanuman Tibba opposite us, climbed by the famous Italian, Riccardo Cassin, made our own objective seem humble in comparison. Nevertheless Ladakhi Peak at 18,000ft/5,500 metres towering above us, looked quite hard enough thank you. We climbed an easy gully and headed up a fairly broad rib. Matt's old leather boots were pretty useless and we twice had to stop to warm up his feet. At about 14,500ft/4,400 metres we stopped and chopped out a platform for the tent, which we were intending to bring up tomorrow. By the time we had finished this it was late morning and we could see dark, threatening clouds rolling in from the south east. We hurried down to the safety of our shelter. No sooner had we arrived when it started to snow. That night the storm reached its peak and at one point lightning was flashing, on average, every ten seconds. Avalanches thundered down nearby Hanuman Tibba – frightening yet exciting. The sheer volume of snow that fell was incredible, and at 3.30 a.m. we decided there was a clear and present danger of us being buried alive. Sleepily and in sub zero temperatures we donned our gear and forced our way out into the thigh deep drifts. For an hour and a half, by the light of our head torches, we worked to clear the tent, a process that was to be repeated many times in the hours that followed. After forty five hours in the tent, and with the consolidated snow four feet deep around us and still falling we decided we had to leave. The food would soon enough run out and we might as well abandon our attempt at Ladakhi Peak. At 8.30 a.m. on 25th April we packed, took down the tent and prepared to leave. Already Matt's feet were feeling numb and I spent time warming them on my bare stomach

– an act that is easy to state in a sentence but involved considerable pain and suffering on both our parts!

Now began our bid to escape, and frankly we had just not considered how desperate it was going to be to re-climb the one thousand feet back to the top of the moraine. Besides his cold feet, Matt was not feeling too good and complained of a thumping headache and slight dizziness. Breaking trail involved me ploughing a way uphill minus my heavy rucksack, with snow sometimes chest deep, consolidating steps for fifty yards at a time, returning first for my sack, and then returning to pick up Matt's sack as he seemed 'out-of-it'. We stopped a few times to dump more and more of our food and petrol in the hope of lightening the loads. As we gained height so the cloud rolled in and everything became a 'white-out'. The experience was very frightening as it was impossible to distinguish features of any kind. We had no sense of up or down, never mind which direction we were heading in. I took my goggles off in the hope it would help, and we floundered blindly on, falling over frequently. By great good fortune our navigational instincts brought us out of the cloud at exactly the right place and we knew we would now live to fight another day. We flogged through the continuing snow, which first turned to sleet and then to rain as we reached the forested valley below. Ten hours after starting we collapsed into a tea shop in the nearest village of Palchan, thoroughly and utterly exhausted.

In this wrecked state we were befriended by a slightly worse for wear Sherpa, one Mr. Bholaram, who took pity on us. He cajoled us back to his house, weaving his way through the narrow alleys, joking with everyone we met, and chasing some pretty girls who fled laughing. We had to force our way through a flock of sheep and goats in his yard, before removing our shoes to climb the stepped ladder, hewn from a log, to the first floor living quarters of his traditional wooden house. Entering his living room we sat on the earth floor and truly felt like honoured guests. A tin stove in the centre of the room belched smoke which tried vainly to escape through the practically non-existent chimney. The room was black, and hanging from the rafters was a half decomposed head of a sheep. It was hanging there, our Sherpa friend said, to remind them that it had been killed by a bear. We were served first tea and later a meal of rice and curried potato. An old man sat in the corner smoking a hubble bubble, raw local tobacco with a lump of burning charcoal on top.

I tried it and it nearly finished me off. There were four women, loads of children and quite a few men who drifted in and out, all remarkably happy. Our new friend then dug around in some boxes and came out with photos, certificates and letters of testimonial from all the many expeditions he had been on. He was clearly a top Sirdar of quite some local renown. Last year, he told me, he had been climbing on Nun Kun, the peak in Ladakh that my father had tried to climb in 1946. Finally it dawned on our hosts that the two young Englishmen were staying awake only by a thread, and they lent us sleeping bags and a room, open to a verandah. We slept on the floor in our wet clothes only because we were just too tired to take them off. The last thing I remember was the sound of singing and drums in another part of the village. Tomorrow there was to be a festival in the village square.

Mr. Bholaram, Solang Nala valley.

CHAPTER 2

Better Luck Next Time

IN THE MORNING WE DISCOVERED that one of Matt's big toes had swollen rather dramatically. When he had been in the south of India two weeks before he had stepped on a thorn, and now it had turned septic. Matt hurried off down to Manali in search of a doctor, and I stayed in the village of Palchan as our new friend Bholaram had practically insisted that I attend their annual festival as his honoured guest. It took some while for my Indian friend and I to reach the village square as all the men he met wanted us to stop and have a drink. I stayed in control, he did not. The rough stone-flagged square, when we had struggled up the hill to it, was a mass of villagers singing and dancing. The square was flanked by old timber and stone houses with large thinly cut slabs of rock as roof tiles. The men dancing in a circle wore white costumes that oddly resembled Greek national costume. Bholaram proudly claimed his people were a remnant of Alexander the Great's

Solang village festival, Kulu. Descendants of Alexander's army?

army. Alexander had certainly passed through Baltistan, quite a distance to the west, however, maybe some of his soldiers made it this far, who knows. Certainly there are many tribes-people in the western Himalaya who claim descent from Alexander's army. Drums beat, the sun shone through ragged clouds, the elders sat in the best places and the women went round topping up the alcohol. Toddlers in dirty, patched clothes, with neck amulets to ward off ill health, played in muddy puddles. Long-haired Himalayan goats, sheep and chickens added to the din and the mess, as food went the rounds. Everyone took a keen and genuine, friendly interest in the young white man, and in the end the men even had me dancing in the circle, much to everyone's amusement.

Two weeks passed. Matt had fled India, where they had wanted to cut off his toe, and returned to England eventually to recover. For me there was an empty, unfulfilled feeling. I had not achieved anything. There was no point in returning until I had stood on top of a decent Himalayan peak. By extremely lucky coincidence another climber, on the edge of the Bristol climbing scene, Roland Perriment, who I knew quite well, turned up in Manali. He and another climber, Paul Bean, were there as an advance party for an expedition that had come to attempt a series of 20,000ft/6,000 metre peaks near the Restricted Area of Spiti to the east. I was told though that there was not room for me to join them. Instead Roland introduced me to a climbing Sirdar friend of his, Rinzing Ladakhi Sherpa, who he said would probably guide me up

Rinzing Ladakhi Sherpa (right), 1977.

the peak Matt and I had just retreated from.

Rinzing had insisted that I come and live at his house near the Buddhist monastery. I remember at the time that I could not believe how utterly genuine he was in his unselfish friendship. He was looking for no gain, and by now, having thrashed my way across India on a shoestring, I was used to seeing a con in every approach to me. He was the first 'Sherpa' Sirdar I was ever to employ in the Himalaya and I did not know it at the time, but there would be other connections in later years. I was unaware until twenty years later that he was close friends with the exiled reincarnate ruler of the small kingdom of Bhutan. This principality lies a thousand miles away at the eastern end of the Himalaya. The exiled ruler, known by the title of the 'Shabdrung', lived close by Rinzing in Manali. He had been introduced to the Shabdrung by his uncle the Rinpoche lama of Stakna monastery in Ladakh. The 'Land of the Lamas', as Ladakh is often called, is a Tibetan Buddhist region just north of the Greater Himalaya. In the early 1600s the king of Ladakh and the very first ruler of Bhutan (the first Shabdrung) had an alliance, and the king of Ladakh had given the Shabdrung lands on which to build Bhutanese monasteries. Rinzing's uncle, the Stakna Rinpoche, was the lama in charge of these Bhutanese monasteries and therefore paid allegiance to the exiled ruler. Most of them still exist to this day.

Rinzing had been born and brought up in Ladakh but later, as a young man, had moved to Manali to find work. He had married a local woman, built a house, and occasionally found work as a porter/guide for expeditions visiting the area.

Twenty nine years later I visited Rinzing at his house and like every Tibetan Buddhist family Rinzing had a shrine room. In pride of place was a photo of his friend the late Shabdrung, who bore an incredible similarity to the first ruler of Bhutan whose stylised image is seen in every monastery in Bhutan. Tucked into the picture frame were two joined identical prints of the newly found reincarnation of the Shabdrung. He was a remarkable looking child who had the rare and unusual physical mark of silver hair around the whorl on the back of his head. He told me that the new Shabdrung, the young boy, had just been taken into protective care by the King of Bhutan and was living in Thimphu, after having been 'recognised' by the Dalai Lama. Without a thought Rinzing took down the double print and with a pair of scissors cut it in half and gave me one of the two pictures.

Rinzing agreed to come and climb Ladakhi peak with me for thirty five rupees per day plus food. However, before we could set out again there was a frustrating period of prolonged bad weather, which felt at the time like it was never going to stop. I eked out my dwindling funds in the run down cafes on the ramshackle main street. Manali itself would never win any architectural prizes, but the people! They came to trade here from Lahoul, Ladakh, Kishtwar and Kashmir. There were also Tibetan refugees living in abject poverty, and Westerners living the hippy life. Many of these stoned Westerners rented houses in the villages in the summer and then migrated to Goa in the winter, taking with them quantities of hash to sell. They would come back the following year with 'acid' and lurid stories of a paradisiacal existence on the white sands of southern India. I met many of them in town and at the nearby hot springs. Some made a bit of money by legitimate trading between Europe and India, some squirreled away hash in secret compartments of cheap souvenirs which they posted to 'safe' addresses, and some got into trouble with the local police. There was a constant paranoia that the police were in league with the local dealers, who sold the drugs, and who then shopped the unsuspecting hippy to the police for a further cut of the bribes, or confiscated substances. I steered clear of the worst of them. Some were like me, they had put real life on 'hold' to experience freedom, travel and adventure – stoned a little but not 'burnt out'. There were professional Indian conmen too, and one learnt to recognise them. One wanted to sell me his tame monkey which did tricks and saluted like a soldier. All of them wanted to buy my watch.

There were further bouts of illness during which Rinzing fussed over me like a mother hen, and shopping trips to the bazaar to buy food for our next attempt on Ladakhi Peak. First though I bussed and walked to the top of the still snowbound pass, the Rotang La, 13,500ft/4,100 metres at the head of the Kulu valley. This is the famous pass which early explorers had used to gain access to the western Himalaya. I had heard traders were crossing the pass now, and that the views from the top were spectacular. Even in winter people cross, when they can, through the snow from Lahoul, to trade in Manali. I was amazed to find on the very top of the pass, buried up to its roof in snow, a rough stone built tea-house serving chai no matter what the weather. It was horribly exhausting wading through wet snow just to reach the pass, and later I missed the last bus back to Manali. Some kind Indian shop keeper gave me a bed for the night at the hamlet of Muri, at the foot of the pass.

The weather was improving, or so it seemed, and when I returned from the Rotang I was overjoyed to find the rest of Roland and Paul's lot had arrived and, having been consulted, they had invited me to join them. They were due to start off in about a week. We agreed there was still just time for me to have another crack at Ladakhi Peak. I was confident now. Having bought Matt's half share of the tent, and food for ten days in the market, I set off with Rinzing on the battered, vomit-covered local bus. Ordinary village folk rarely travel in any kind of motor vehicle and when they do the twisting road, and the swaying, bumping bus soon induces travel sickness. Add also the fact that Indian buses are always packed with humanity, goats and sheep, with more folk on the roof and hanging off the sides and it meant we had to fight for standing room. It has always mystified me how it is that these shoddy, beaten-up contraptions ever make it for hundreds of miles over the highest passes in the world, on rotten roads, and carrying double their maximum load.

At the road head we hired a porter and set off in glorious sunshine retracing our earlier steps. We met an Austrian couple who were making a wildlife film and planning to capture a bear. I wished them the best of luck, secretly thinking they must be mad. Later we met two village men returning from a hunting trip. This time I was secretly pleased they were empty handed. Lastly we exchanged pleasantries with a bumptious Indian government officer whose manservant held an umbrella over his master's head. What he was doing up there I never did find out. In any case on that first evening, there were sure signs of more bad weather on the way, and to add to my worries I was up half the night with a reoccurrence of my stomach trouble.

Dawn brought completely overcast skies and though feeling ill and weak I decided to carry on. Midway through the morning, just cresting a rise, I came upon Rinzing and our porter crouched down behind a large rock. They waved me over. Fingers on pursed lips showed the need for silence. There, some one hundred yards away, on the opposite bank of a stream were three large brown bears. They were blissfully unaware of our presence until Rinzing with a mischievous grin gave a yell. Three noses sniffed the air and for a good few minutes they just stared at us. Then they ran uphill beating a retreat into the forest. It was a steep, long hillside and they simply sprinted up it. I understood from that moment on that even the fittest man would stand no chance of outrunning a bear. By midday it had started to snow and we could see no more than three hundred yards. It is a truly miserable experience to have a dose of the shits in sub-zero temperatures and a blizzard, and finally we simply turned round and headed back down. It was deeply depressing but I could console myself with the thought that I had tried my best, and that I could now look forward to the real expedition with Roland.

On 12th May five of us set off in pursuit of Paul and Roland who had gone in advance to secure porters and mules, and to set up Base Camp. We survived another bus journey that set the standard for all future Himalayan bus journeys I was ever to make. We charged along a dirt road teetering on the edges of several abysses with the local passengers seemingly oblivious to the mortal danger they were in. The road was so rough that on one occasion we went over a particularly bad pothole and everyone hit the ceiling. I have this vision of everyone suspended in mid air before they crashed back into their seats, rubbing the top of their heads and carrying on talking.

I had not been to the toilet for a week, not since the blizzard, and when the bus stopped I was in great pain. Frankly, constipation is worse than breaking bones. That day I crapped five times and all of it solid. It is quite astonishing how much material the body can store away! In any case we were relieved to be walking again and shortly came to the beautiful small town of Manikarin with its hot springs, two temples, and steaming water running in gutters down the side of the main street. We chose to camp some way beyond and were going to sleep in the open until we discovered a scorpion and a large ugly looking spider on the ground.

Five more days through glorious mountain country and Lord of the Rings type villages, carrying rucksacks that tested our youthful strength to the limit, brought us to our Base Camp on the East Toss glacier at 14,000ft/4,250 metres. Here we were to stay for three weeks of intense climbing activity. Now I really felt I had properly arrived in the Himalaya. Peerless peaks surrounded us on all sides, and avalanches occasionally thundered down vertiginous mountain faces. We were quite safe from them, parked in the centre of the glacier, but initially at least we scrambled out of our tents each time to watch the spectacle. The weather too had settled into a pattern of clear, bitterly cold nights, sunny mornings, and snow showers in the afternoons. We excitedly pored over maps identifying peaks, discussing possible climbing routes, and Paul Bean, the expedition leader, showed us what had already been done in the area and what was still virgin. We talked, we planned, we calculated food supplies and we moulded as a team. We watched each others' fitness, and in a subtle English way jockeyed for position at the starting gate.

First though for several days we ferried loads to an Advance Base Camp at the foot of a mountain called White Sail, 21,128ft. The route was unknown, untried and after climbing a ridge next to an icefall Paul, Roland and Tara tentatively roped across the Papsura glacier thankfully avoiding falling into any crevasses. Up there the air was thin, the sun during the day almost intolerably hot, and at night the temperature plummeted to minus fifteen degrees centigrade. The build up and the banter had been relaxed, the decisions straightforward. Hard work but not frightening, but now the days that lay ahead would be real climbing to altitudes in excess of 20,000ft/6,000 metres. I guess we were too young to realise the dangers. Summit fever had us firmly in its grip. Our first plan was that Paul, Tara Chand and Barry Needle would attempt Devachan, a virgin peak of 20,300ft/6,188 metres to the north, while Roland, George and I would try the first ascent of the South West Ridge of White Sail. The climb was to be another major disappointment for me. Although I felt strong and fit I suffered my first experience of high altitude sickness. We climbed a steep gully, then through rocks at the top, and finally Roland hacked his way through a cornice to reach a plateau at 18,500ft/5,650 metres but by then my head pounded with unrelenting pain, I felt dizzy, and crossing the short distance to a campsite in the searing heat left me totally exhausted. Squashed into our tent that night I shivered uncontrollably, could not sleep, and found that Asprin was not man enough to banish the thumping headache. So close and yet so far; in the morning my new found friends unselfishly gave up the summit to shepherd me back down the steep icy slopes to camp.

As we staggered into Advance Base the others came out to carry our sacks the last yards and we heard of their success on Devachen. At the very least the expedition had achieved a summit. The very next day Roland and Barry went back to try White Sail again, but still needing further time to acclimatise I returned all the way to Base Camp with George Crawford-Smith, feeling particularly depressed, in worsening weather. It snowed hard, we ate a lot of food, and I helped George with his mapping. Load carrying was something useful to do and on returning to Advance we were in time to join some of the others in an ascent of a virgin 18,000ft/5,500 metres peak to the east of White Sail. While we had been away Roland and Barry had climbed above the bad weather that had enveloped Advance Base, and they enjoyed the privilege of seeing a forest of Himalayan peaks rising out of a perfect sea of cloud. Theirs was the second ascent of White Sail in the forty million years or so of its existence.

This time on the virgin peak I felt fine as we hacked our way up the

South Face of White Sail's satellite, and gingerly traversed its knife- edged summit. We named it Jubilation Peak for obvious reasons, twenty five years on from the coronation of Queen Elizabeth II. From its precarious summit we had seen another strikingly beautiful mountain, Angdu Ri, 19,530ft/5,953 metres, to the north east. Its sprawling bulk and fine ridges attracted me; it seemed the next logical objective, my last chance to be able to return home with a reasonably major peak to my credit. On the same day that George and I set out for Angdu Ri, Roland and Barry, acclimatised and fit, had also set out to try a first ascent of the South West Ridge of Papsura, 21,164ft/6,451 metres, the highest peak in the region. This ridge dominated the view above Advance Base. The more it was scrutinised the greater the ambition became to give it a try.

By now we reckoned to have only four days' food left at Advance Base and we could all see that Papsura's South West Ridge would involve hard rock-climbing, followed by a long snow ridge to the summit. The descent could not be seen as it lay on the other side of the mountain, though it had been studied during the ascent of Devachen. None of us had any misgivings or doubts, it was worth a try. How often in life ambition outstrips common sense. We were flush with our successes. Were we now not making enough allowance for the unforeseen? The main feature was about to start on Papsura, and George and I were playing in the B movie. Nevertheless I was in a state of childlike excitement at the prospect of heading off up a peak nearly twenty thousand feet, just the two of us, with a few days' food and a small tent.

Mt Angdu Ri, 19,500ft, East Toss glacier, Himachal Pradesh as seen from the summit of Jubilation Peak.

Looking at it now, nearly thirty years later, perhaps I see Angdu Ri a little through rose tinted spectacles. However, our two visits to the summit were extraordinary experiences. George and I had climbed all day, past Jubilation Peak, and after one steep snow and ice face had gained a ridge leading to the summit. Just as we reached the final cone of rocks we found a perfect ledge for our tent so instead of heading for the top we erected it, had a sleep and waited for the sunset. It had been hot as we climbed laboriously upwards but the afternoon clouds brought a snow shower which then rattled the tent. However, around dusk it stopped and we emerged. I remember being stunned by the sight below us. I urged George to hurry and scrambling to the highest point we literally marvelled at the view. The remains of the small storm were drifting through the mountains below us, a patchwork of broken clouds moving as if drawn on a string. White Sail, our neighbour, blotted out the view to the north west but in every other direction glaciers and ice clad giants reached out to every horizon. As the sun sank into the cotton wool to the west I took photos that ever since I have been thrilled to look at. God then took out his painting set and shaded the edges of the earth subtle pinks and purples as we stood and shivered, and the temperature plummeted. We stayed up there until it required head torches to find our way down fifty feet to our single skin tent.

Off with crampons, hands numb, and one at a time we crawled into our tiny tunnel tent to fumble, curse and wriggle into our 'pits'. Into the sleeping bags with us went the soft inner boots, the water bottles and the cameras to stop them freezing. Then, one person kneeling to coax our petrol stove into life, we melted snow for drinks, cooked a simple meal, and lastly George set the alarm. We had decided that we just had to see the sunrise. We closed our sleeping bags so that only our noses were exposed, and settled down for a cold night. At pre-dawn we were grumpily up and heading for the small rocky platform on the summit again. Our hard sacrifice of leaving the relatively warm sleeping bags was fair exchange for the unexpected magic show that followed. It was so cold I narrowed my mouth to a thin slit to allow air in more slowly; I was worried it would freeze my lungs, and we waited. Was that the horizon or what was it? As the sky lightened, the unrisen sun cast a shadow of the earth into the atmosphere just above the horizon. To begin with it was quite a broad band but as we neared dawn the black line above the horizon narrowed, and then a fine pointed shape appeared within the shadow. The sun's rays rising directly behind our mountain were diffracted somehow forming a pyramidal shape within the earth's shadow. Neither of us had ever heard of such a phenomonom before and were profoundly amazed. As the sun finally touched our faces and made the snow at our feet sparkle like diamonds, the shadow disappeared.

It was a place where none of life's worries could touch me; there was only the sublime ancient beauty of the mountains. Whilst in the world of men armies had come and gone, dynasties had risen and fallen, momentous events in history had happened and then been forgotten, the mountains had barely changed in forty million years; eight times as long as man has existed. All that had happened where I then crouched gazing in wonder, was that the sun had come and gone, snow had fallen and melted, and the stars had moved their positions fractionally. Man had been there only twice.

I later discovered that the first ascent of Angdu Ri had been made by Rinzing and named after his eldest son, Angdu.

We knew only too well that once the sun had been up for only a few hours the hard frozen crust, that easily bore a man's weight, would soften. Once that happened each step was treble the effort, and by midday you would be sinking up to your knees. We packed the tent and hurried down to the tiny dots three and a half thousand feet below.

Back in camp we joined Paul, Dawn and Tara Chand to watch events unfold on Papsura, through binoculars. Roland and Barry could be seen as tiny dots moving barely perceptibly up the rock ridge. As clouds rolled in at 6.30 p.m. they disappeared from view. At 8.15 p.m. we saw some flashes high on the ridge. Surely it was not their distress flare. Then nothing.

Next morning there was no sign of life. Not at 6.00 a.m., nor at 7.00 a.m. when the sun hit Advance Base Camp. Finally at 8.30 a.m. we thought we could see them moving down. What was wrong – was one of them ill or injured? But no, they moved up again. Then it took them an hour to go up one hundred feet, but by 11.00 a.m. they had finished the rock-climbing and were inching their way up the sharp snow ridge towards the summit. Then they disappeared from view, only to reappear above a bergschrund. Our jangling nerves relaxed a little and at 1.05 p.m. Advance Base Camp erupted in shouts of elation as we saw them stand on the very top. At 2.25 p.m. however a thunderstorm moved in and snow started to fall heavily. The weather was beginning to break up, as for some time we had suspected it might. Later in the afternoon Paul and Tara roped out across the glacier to see if they could see any sign of them, but the wind and the snow obliterated their own tracks, and even they had a tricky time finding their way back to us. At 7.00 a.m. the next morning Paul, George and myself set out to see if we could find them.

We looked up Papsura's southern gully, the way we had expected them to descend, and not a sign. No little black dots or signs of tracks. Paul thought perhaps they might have tried to climb down the untried North West Ridge in the storm, so Paul and I went further up the glacier to look, leaving George to keep watch over the southern gully. We were by now beginning to fear the worst. They should definitely have appeared long ago.

Such wonderful relief then when we saw them coming towards us from the direction of the North West Ridge. Back in camp with the cookers going non-stop producing endless cups of tea, they related their story.

After their bivouac at the foot of the climb they had soloed steep snow slopes leading to the start of the ridge proper. Crossing these slopes Barry had slipped, but had stopped a fatal fall by braking with his ice axe, sliding only twenty feet before stopping. All this went unseen by Roland out in front. After three hours of interconnected snow slopes they had started rock-climbing up solid granite. Short walls, slabs and towers were slowly linked together, but the place where they thought they might be able to stop for the night proved impossible, and they had been forced to carry on. One impasse after another, fearfully exposed pitches on the very rim of the ridge, and climbing so hard even Barry had asked for a tight rope. It was getting late in the afternoon, darkness was not far off and still they were confronted by hard climbing. A tension traverse across a blank wall, a steep corner filled with snow, a chimney choked with unstable snow and ice. Then above and to the right they spotted a ledge under an overhang. It was big enough to sleep on but there was no room for the tent. There was space for one person to lie down and for the other to sit. The flashes we had seen from below were their efforts in persuading the stove to light in sub-zero temperatures. Having hammered in some pitons they clipped on and got what sleep they could.

In the morning only three pitches of snow-covered rock remained before the snow arête to the summit. Exhausted and thirsty they shared a tin of sardines and ate snow to quench their raging thirst. They could see the storm approaching and hurried off the summit. After two rope lengths it had started to snow. In the gathering gloom they headed down towards a snowfield where they thought they might be able to pitch a tent to sit out the storm, but it was too steep and they had to carry on. Wet gloves froze, beards and clothing became caked in ice and then they had hit mirror smooth ice. Conscious of huge drops to the left they cramponed down. They saw a break in the cliffs below and hoping for shelter carried on down. By then it was 6.00 p.m. and again darkness was not far off. Spindrift avalanches then threatened to sweep them down more steep slopes. Not being able to see very far through the driving snow and cloud they knew they must find a way to the glacier at the bottom and somewhere to pitch the tent or they were going to freeze to death. A bergschrund appeared and they jumped past its lip into soft snow below. Now they dared hope they were safe; the glacier lay below and although the spindrift avalanches were by now almost continuous they quickly made their way to a flat, safe spot out on the glacier. The tent, still frozen solid, was put up with difficulty and they crawled inside. Their outer clothes and climbing gear were all left outside in the snow. They ate some chocolate bars, biscuits and some nuts, and struggled into their still damp sleeping bags. The wind got up in the night making life unpleasant and in their exhausted state they had not surfaced until late in the morning, which is when we met them slowly weaving down the glacier, avoiding the crevasses.

It was over. By now high altitude, and freeze dried rations, had produced skeletal replicas of our previous selves. We were starving, and back in Base Camp we gorged ourselves on as much food as we could consume. We ate so much we had painful stomachs. It seemed there were endless sessions of making chapatis over full throated Primus stoves. We were finished with blisters, burnt tongues, split lips, peeling noses, chapped thighs, headaches, brittle nails, cuts that did not heal, matted hair, smelly farts, stinking feet and dirty clothes. We wanted to stock up on beer, cigarettes, hot showers, music, laughter and curry.

Our food and time had run out, and we withdrew to the snout of the East Toss Glacier to rendezvous with the horsemen. We walked and ran back to the fleshpots of India, our senses shocked by the smells and sights of green grass and flowers. Back to the haggling, hustling, humid streets of Manali where people struggle to make a living from one day to the next. Back on the vomit-covered bus across the plains of India to frenetic Delhi where the temperature was in the mid forties Centigrade. Where you could drink a can of Coke and watch it a minute later emerge as sweat on your arms. Where at night without air conditioning in your hotel room the only way of keeping remotely comfortable was to pour cold water from the fridge onto the bed sheets and get back into bed. To rickshaws, curry, hot showers and emporiums crammed with irresistible Indian artefacts. To lazy days with a good book in the Lodi gardens where it was fun to watch the world go by, and finally a return on the big bird back to family, friends and the prospect of finding a new job. Being wild and free again in the mountains had to wait.

CHAPTER 3

Towards the Crystal Willow

WHAT STARTED IT ALL FOR ME was a black and white photograph[1] on the stairs at my gran's house in Yorkshire. In the days before motorways, computers and before man had landed on the moon we used to drive from Oxford to stay with gran and the two aunts, Ada and Gladys. In those days it was a different world up there. Accents were broad, lorries belched clouds of black smoke, coal and steel were still massive industries, trams ran in Huddersfield and when we looked down from gran's house across Brighouse there was a forest of tall mill chimneys. The budgie swore and the Hoover with a light scared me so much I hopped onto the settee to escape it, but the thing I remember the most was the photo. A black 'A' frame tent with a pair of someone's boot soles poking out of the entrance, an ice axe sticking in the snow outside, and behind, the steep face of a mountain wreathed in thin cloud. In dad's scrawl the magic words 'Nun Kun, Ladakh, India. Camp III (20,000ft). June '46 (Stobart inside tent)'. I still have that photo.

If it was dad's axe it had belonged to Spencer Chapman who had used it on the first ascent of Chomolhari, the second highest peak in Bhutan. He had given it to my father, who had in turn donated it to the Himalayan Club after his expedition to Nun Kun. I am sorry to say the axe was never to be seen again. Tom Stobart was dad's climbing partner and later went as the official photographer on the '53 Everest expedition.

I had of course heard dad's stories of Nun Kun dozens of times, but I never bored of them, though I often pretended I did. The one about how he had had one of his back teeth removed by pliers and how the morphine only worked an hour after the tooth had been extracted. Of how he had saved Stobart's life after he had slipped down an ice slope, by hauling him up before he fell over a cliff, of how they had failed to climb Nun because their cookers had packed up, and how after climbing White Needle Peak,

---

1 See back cover.

one of Nun's subsidiaries, he had gone hunting a bear. They had practically run out of food but instead of the bear he had shot an ibex. At the same time he told us of how he had stumbled upon a huge monastery where the lamas had never seen a white man before, and how the head monk had presented him with a crystal, a slate engraved with a mantra, and a prayer wheel.

However the dreams of finishing the job off for the Old Man by climbing Nun with my brother Richard, and five other friends, had to submit to the reality of life. I needed to try and find a respectable job. At interviews my would-be employers only wanted to talk about my climbs in the Himalaya. At the interview for the job I really wanted, my boss had hitched to India as a spotty youth and we immediately hit it off. I knuckled down to working for an old established firm of surveyors for three and a half years. To be honest I enjoyed it, though it really wasn't me. I was never interested in the career path, the political manoeuvring to partnership, the large car, the ever larger house. All my friends were climbers and all my spare time was spent rock-climbing and partying. So we planned, we scrounged free gear, applied for grants from stuffy old institutions, we attracted the local BBC to the idea of a short film to be shot by ourselves, and the day finally came to hand in my letter of resignation. I am sure my boss was envious.

The heat on the platform at Delhi threatened to overwhelm me. Crowds jostled and shouted. All manner of races, creeds and colours; rich corpulent men full of their own importance, Belsen-like beggar men pulling at your heart strings, men in pyjamas, men in suits, women hidden by yashmaks, beautiful sexy women in silk saris too shy even to catch your eye, porters in grubby red uniforms grabbing at our bags. It was a shocking cross section of humanity; some asleep on charpoys, others queuing for tickets for tomorrow's train, everyone sweating, arguing and kow-towing to bureaucracy. How could anyone think sanely, I wondered, in this abominable heat. Up went the cry "Gharam chai, gharam chai" from the platform tea sellers and yet strangely, by some miracle of physics, boiling hot tea was actually refreshing.

Inside our eight berth sleeper compartment eight of us, including our Liason Officer, celebrated with a bottle of Glorious Twelfth scotch. We were crammed in amongst eight bulging rucksacks and ten large boxes of expedition gear. The steel box was an oven, with bars. Eventually the steam train whistled and jarringly edged out of the station. An Indian friend Rene waved and smiled knowingly. After half an hour we may have accelerated to twenty miles per hour, and either it was boil to death inside but be happily drunk, or sit on the roof and eat soot. The latter was the better option, and the braver of us strode along the roofs of the carriages jumping James Bond style from one to the next. Indiaaahhhh flowed past, and teeth to the wind we revelled in the wild experience. Steam trains, bullock drawn carts, dusty villages, people by the side of the track nodding their heads from side to side and laughing and waving at us, peacocks in the fields for hour after hour after hour.

The train made mournful sounds into the night and stopped frequently to re-hydrate. An attendant appeared early in the morning with some suspect curry for breakfast. Travelling across India with an expedition is a never ending series of arguments with taxi drivers, bus conductors, lorry owners and rickshaw people who, once they see you are at their mercy for transport, use every possible means to extract the highest possible price. Arrival at Jammu station was a classic. Prolonged negotiations with the railway porters were followed by use of the back door at the bus station ticket office. Extra money secured the tickets but then the bus driver would not take our luggage. We paid him extra and still he would not take it. By now a full scale crowd had gathered; fifty or sixty people all shouting and gesticulating. The station manager had the last word and wanted one hundred rupees. We settled for twenty five, shook hands with those who minutes earlier had been calling us all the names under the sun and off we went.

Twelve hours later grinding down through the gears, and making full use of the triple air horns, we dropped out of the foothills into the Vale of Kashmir. It is a paradise of green paddy fields and wooded countryside spoilt only by religion. Our friend in Delhi, Alok Chandola, an ex-aide to the President of India and school chum of Rajiv Gandhi, had given us a contact in Srinagar. His name was Gafoor Wahid, a young cheerful man though nearly blind, and he owned a fine bungalow in three or four acres of orchard. At Srinagar bus station the police eventually cleared the crowd of hustlers and taxi drivers and we drove to Gafoor's place. Here we stayed for a few days while we met the Director of Tourism for J & K State, then the Deputy Director for J & K Road Transport, and then Major Bathwal who was the officer in charge of 'Beacons'. This was the name of the regiment responsible for maintenance of the road from Kashmir to Ladakh. We had hoped to drive from Srinagar over the Zoji La pass to the town of Kargil, and from there up into the Suru valley to begin our trek to the Base Camp. However, the Zoji La was still snowbound and although the army had just got one truck through, the authorities would not allow us to try.

These were interesting days where we learnt how polite, correct and hospitable Indian upper echelons like to be, how frustrating and time consuming it is to extract decisions, and how perfectly beautiful are the lakes of Kashmir. The rides through the lily fields and reeds, with their kingfishers, multi-hued ducks, egrets, floating islands, stilt houses and boats powered by heart shaped paddles felt an almost indecent indulgence. We also learnt the art of 'blanking out' even the most persistent hustlers, who if they noticed even the flick of an eye in their direction would parade an interminable morass of trinkets from dozens of aluminium trunks in the bottoms of their boats, until you bought something just to get rid of them.

Lingering there would no doubt have won a secret ballot but we decided to fly on to Leh, capital of Ladakh, on the weekly flight instead of losing another week with no guarantee that the road would open. With incredible naivety we turned up for the flight not imagining that our seven hundred kilograms of equipment and food would be any problem. Our youthful exuberance, impeccable credentials and brazen smooth talking persuaded the ground crew to accept the lot at no charge. We really felt at last we were getting the hang of travel in India.

Five minutes after take off we were over snowy mountains as far as the eye could see. I admit to a certain anxiousness and hoped the plane would not develop a fault. Off in the left-hand middle distance were spotted K2, Nanga Parbat, Masherbrum and Gasherbrum, the giants of the Karakoram, while on the right side was our mountain Nun and its sister peak Kun, so close we could pick out every detail. This precious time was all too short as our jet seemed to creep past the massif's huge bulk.

Views of Mt Nun on the flight from Srinagar to Leh.

We crowded together pointing out the details of the climb to come. The captain called me into his cockpit to film; it seemed the whole plane was joining in with the excitement of our climb. Then the plane started its descent into the desolate valley next to the Indus river. When the first plane had landed at Leh many years ago, the people from surrounding areas thought it was a god from the sky and had brought offerings to placate the monster, and hay for it to feed on. Steep turns with glimpses of serrated rocky ridges dangerously close, coupled with the view of a Potala-like monastery and we had landed to cheers and clapping.

A tin shed served as an airport arrivals hall and by now we were becoming used to the triplicate form filling procedure. The air felt thin and dry. We were now standing at eleven thousand five hundred feet. Yet again we had a special introduction from Alok; this time to Mr. Wangchuk Kalon, whose family had been ministers in the time of the kings of Ladakh. They now owned one of the oldest hotels in the town, the Kang Lhha Chen, to which we retreated.

Spread around Leh, and a few miles only from the river Indus, lay a patchwork quilt of multicoloured cultivated fields. At their edges desert stretched as far as the eye could see. To the north the mountains shut off the Restricted Area of Nubra, and the old trading route to Yarkand and beyond. Across the river you could see a string of oases dotted at the foot of alluvial fans. South again was the pointed snow peak of Stok Kangri. Unbeknown to me it was later to play a pivotal role in my life. Just then it was the highest peak visible in the Zanskar range.

Leh is dominated by a palace said to have been designed by the same architect who worked on the Potala in Lhasa. Legend has it that he was either having an affair with the king's wife, or had been embezzling from his coffers, but the result was that he had had his hands chopped off. Others say it was so that he could not take his designs to another rival kingdom. Wangchuk pointed out the holes in the walls where Zowara Singh, from Kashmir, had shelled the palace in 1837, forcing the king's abdication. The rather stark and dusty town at its foot was a shocking contrast to the graceful shikaras skimming across the silk smooth lakes of Srinagar, with its perfect reflections of the surrounding snow-capped mountains, poplar trees, and the remains of the Mogul gardens. Here the people wore thick dark purple gowns like the Tibetans, stove pipe hats, and footwear I thought existed only in history books – knee high boots with turned up toes and made of felt and rope. Later as we walked about the town an old tough-looking man walked up to us and repeatedly saluted. Was he being funny, was he a little crazy, or was he saying 'we respect the mighty British Empire and haven't forgotten you ruled India until recently.'? I think it was a little of each. Any physical effort left us gasping for air, and you just knew the sun was doing you damage.

News of our arrival in town spread quickly and that first evening we received a deputation of the town's taxi drivers. They wanted the job of driving us two days to the roadhead in the Suru valley, and they said we would need three jeeps. The price was exorbitant. A lorry driver appeared and offered to take us all for one seventh of the cost of just one of the taxis. Another mighty row broke out. The taxi drivers claimed it was illegal for the lorry driver to take passengers. This slight difference of opinion was only resolved by taking the dispute before the local Chief Superintendent of Police. We ended up with one lorry and two jeeps. By the evening I had developed a thumping headache and I left my brother Richard and some of the others still wrangling over the price, while I went to sleep.

The next day we were up at 3.30 a.m. for the eight hour drive to Kargil. The early start was to beat the army convoys which often blocked the tortuous road in the summer. We were sorry to leave the magical city of Leh with its red-robed monks, Buddhist shrines and Tibetan-looking people. Ladakhis long to be independent again. The State of Jammu and Kashmir is now their political master, and everyone we met had stories of the corruption of their Kashmiri overlords. In days of old they had been a powerful independent kingdom, whose kings were direct descendants from Tibet's early royal family, but then came Zowarar Singh and after him the British, and finally India took over where they left off.

Delicate negotiations with lorry and taxi drivers!   *Photo: Richard Berry*

The road took us over two major passes, the Fotu La, 13,479ft/4,108 metres and the Namika La, 12,500ft/3,810 metres For some of the time we were driving beside the river Indus, at other times through deep gorges; everywhere were arid, rocky, desolate hills with snowy peaks as a backdrop. None of us had ever seen road construction like it. Loop after loop of stacked hairpins climbing up improbable mountainsides, maintained by the army. An un-publicised war was being fought in a gentlemanly way on the Siachen Glacier between Pakistan and India. The road was needed constantly by the Indian army, except in the winter when the two sides retreated by agreement to their respective valleys, until the following spring when they would take up positions, and start shelling each other all over again.

Kargil was, and still is, a dump. Everything about it is ugly and why anyone should choose to live there is beyond understanding. It was regularly shelled from across the border. We were dropped at the only decent place in town, the Tourist Bungalow. Our taxi drivers tried one last time to swindle us out of more money, and tempers on both sides now had reached breaking point. Luckily the friendly Tourist Officer intervened and fetched his friend the local Session Judge to mediate. The amount was agreed but we discovered that we just did not have enough cash. So, at 8 p.m. at night the local bank manager was dug out of his house and sufficient cash was found to pay off the drivers. We heaved a sigh of relief when they drove off into the sunset.

Next day was one of comparative rest, when we purchased our

On the road to Nun.

supply of paraffin, and cashed some money. This involved visiting the bank in the high street; a tatty building that had two soldiers guarding it armed with Enfield rifles. It took hours of form filling and making nonsensical entries into huge moth-eaten ledgers. Finally, we visited the District Commissioner for the State of Jammu and Kashmir. A very pleasant man from whom we learnt that one of the taxi drivers was a known rapist, and he promised to be very unpleasant to him if the occasion and opportunity arose.

We were now on the final leg of our road journey and having got shot of the taxis we all piled into the one remaining lorry, the driver of which was an honest, decent man. He took us bouncing up the rough track towards Panikar in the Suru valley. This is a long, deep, fertile valley and was quite a change from the desert-like scenery of Ladakh. We checked into the police station at Sanko where we signed a register, noting that Micky Mouse had been there before us. Barry posed handcuffed to the local Bobby. We were in high spirits. A little further on we rounded a corner and there was Nun Kun streaming cloud from the twin summits. To this point it had all been light hearted fun and adventure but now the truth of our ambition stood in front of us; gigantic, regal, uncaring of our fate one way or the other. It seemed almost inconceivable that we could stand on the top of the gargantuan. I remember thinking that it was going to be a lot of hard work getting to the top.

Further on and still a couple of miles from the village of Panikar, where we expected to hire horses, the lorry got stuck in a snowdrift.

Lorry stuck in a snowdrift.

The drift, that was slightly higher than the lorry, was the remains of the winter storms and a gap had been cut through for vehicles, but our lorry went charging at the gap and wedged itself against one of the side banks. The driver crawled into the freezing puddle under his lorry trying to jack it up somehow but whatever he tried it remained well and truly stuck fast. By now we had collected a young man called Ghulam Rasool, nephew of the Tourist Officer at Kargil, and son of the Headman at Panikar. Ghulam was going to organise the pack horses and so while we set up camp he walked on to his father's village. We were paying Ghulam personally to take film back to his nephew, who in turn was passing in back to Mark Tully, the BBC correspondent in Delhi, so that he could send it back to regional BBC in Bristol. We hoped that by making sure Ghulam was happy he would keep the porters and horsemen happy for us.

Good to his word Ghulam returned early next morning with eighteen ponies and nine porters for the start of our walk-in. In two days we hoped to reach Gulamantongus where we would leave the jeep track, cross the river, and start the long climb up to Base Camp. While the main party and ponies took the long route round a huge bend in the Suru river, three of us took the 'short-cut' over a thirteen and a half thousand foot pass, the Purkutse La. To do this we had to cross the river on a sagging suspension bridge. In the Old Man's day this bridge was entirely made from interwoven birch twigs. Many sweaty hours later we enjoyed magnificent views of the North Face of Nun from the pass, cloud spewing from her summit like smoke from a factory chimney.

Summit of Nun viewed from the Purkutse La pass.

Below we could see the huge loop that the road made, following the course of the Suru river. Descending from the pass we met up again with the main party and were amazed to meet a friend of John Margesson's, one of our expedition members. This man incredibly had followed us from Delhi, after hearing of our expedition, and delivered to me, as the official leader, a letter from the Indian Mountaineering Foundation concerning one Dr. Mutch. This American gentleman was a space scientist who, in 1980, had disappeared while climbing Nun. The *Daily Telegraph* had reported on its front page that he had been kidnapped by Russians at a height of 22,000ft. Intrigued by this report, and not wishing to end up in a Labour camp in Siberia, I had written to the IMF asking for information. They were keen that we should locate the body and bring it down the mountain.

The road carried on eastwards towards the monastery which dad had stumbled upon, and from there carried on over the Pensi La Pass into the kingdom of Zanskar. Our course was now taking us through breathtakingly beautiful mountain country, past the snout of the mighty Gangri Glacier and on, up a road strewn with massive rockfalls, avalanches and deep snow drifts. We felt sure it would require an army to clear it for the summer months. To our amazement when we came down off the mountain on 2nd July the work had been completed. We had walked up the road on 22nd May. We arrived at Gulamantongus without mishap, knowing that here we had to cross a wide river.

On the following day I nearly got swept away. Although the river was wide it was shallow at this time of the year but only just fordable. The water was exceedingly cold and feet and legs were numb in seconds. It is quite surprising that I was ever again able to perform any conjugal activity. The porters linked arms and went across in a line with their Tibetan style robes hitched up round their waists. There could be no hurrying through the ice cold water as each step with bare feet had to be placed carefully. The pain when circulation returned on the opposite bank was extreme.

We were now following in the footsteps of the famous American explorers, the Bullock-Workmans and stopped at their moraine camp for the night, a long way after the river. During the day some of the porters had come round a bend on the vague mountain path to be confronted by a bear. Luckily it made off, but the porters were in quite a state of agitation that evening. Before I left home I had read a Japanese expedition report which had said their Base Camp had been ransacked by a bear. The report jokingly said the bear had left much of the food untouched but had consumed all their whisky. That had been the previous year so we reasoned it must be the same animal. Of course the bear now knew we were there.

The following day we struggled up the side of the Shaffat Glacier. It was tough, treacherous ground for the horses, and for men. Towards the end of the day the slopes became steeper and I started to complain to Ghulam that I thought it was becoming too hard for the horses. He told me not to worry. In retrospect Ghulam should have refused to take them on, or we should have insisted they turn back. However, what did we know about horses, and as this was their land and their horses it seemed crass to insist. Then as they struggled up a steep slope one of the horses missed its footing and literally somersaulted three or four times down the slope. By luck it was stopped from rolling to its death. The porters seemed to think the horse was at fault and proceeded to turn the air blue with their cursing. It was the last obstacle though, and shortly after, we arrived at the Bullock-Workman's Camp, situated just below the snowline. There were the remains of some fairly substantial old walls, and scraping around we produced some very old tins. Perhaps they belonged to my dad. I shall never know.

We knew by now that there was also a Japanese team camped a day ahead of us who had been attempting to climb Kun, Nun's sister peak. One of the Japanese had become seriously ill with altitude sickness and we had seen the helicopter flying overhead to lift him out. Some Zanskari porters turned up at our camp shortly after us, on their way to evacuate the Japanese team. Several of the Zanskaris wore nothing on their feet and stood around in the snow as though this was nothing unusual. It impressed us enormously.

From the camp we had our first views of Nun from the east, and its magnificent satellite Zanskar 1, still a long, long way away. Nun itself though was an ugly brute seen from this side. The next few days were spent shifting all our kit to Base Camp at 16,250ft/4,953 metres. It was our first taste of really hard work and for the first day we had managed to persuade our nine porters to stay on and help. However, as we had nowhere where they could sleep above the snow line we were forced to pay them off. On arrival we shared a small snow plateau with the Japanese for one night. Unfortunately this forced us to camp in a slight dip, and several days later this turned into a small lake, threatening to make ours the first underwater camp at over 16,000ft.

The nearest phone was five days' march away, the Japanese had bowed repeatedly, hugged us and left, and with great ceremony and many speeches our own porters mimicked the bowing, and returned to Panika laughing. There was, however, one person who also left and who should have stayed, our Liason Officer, Neelam Kumar.

CHAPTER 4

The Drinks Officer and a White Needle

THE LIAISON OFFICER'S JOB WAS SUPPOSED to be to assist us in crossing the Indian sub-continent, and to help us overcome any difficulties we might encounter with local people. Unfortunately as we floundered our way across India Neelam proved not to be a friend and fellow climber, but yet another problem who required ever dwindling supplies of patience and tact. He was a pain in the backside, and I am afraid to say we had grown to dislike and distrust him. Our fears proved to be not unfounded. He bragged about his prowess as a climber, he was lazy, and he considered that his status as our Liason Officer meant that any other staff had to bow and scrape to him. In our first meeting he tried to persuade us that we should use friends of his in Srinagar to handle all the arrangements for the expedition. I had to make it plain that we would make our own arrangements as we went along, or use Alok's contacts. Whenever there were 'delicate' negotiations to be conducted he was nowhere to be seen, or stayed largely in the background. Having claimed he would be coming to the summit with us, the closer we got the more obvious it was to us that he would not. Sure enough on that last day he came to me and asked to be excused the climb. He wanted to go trekking for two weeks he said, and could he borrow 700 rupees, a tent and some equipment. We expressed our deep regret that he had decided not to join us, and asked what we could do to help him on his chosen path. I am sure Neelam did not feel a thing as we bit his arm off!

It later transpired that, having left us, instead of trekking he had returned direct to Srinagar where he stayed eighteen days with our friend Gafoor. He was met four days after arriving in Kashmir by his wife who had travelled up from Delhi to join him, prearranged we were told. Not only did they not pay to stay with Gafoor, or for any of the food that was cooked for them, but he had borrowed a further 200 rupees from our blind friend. We did not see Neelam until we were due to fly home, when he returned the equipment but not the money. He had not repaid Gafoor.

To cover his tracks for returning to Srinagar early he had written a letter to the IMF accusing us of not providing him with his own cook and porter, when in fact he did not carry a single load, not even his personal rucksack, nor did he do any cooking. More fundamental though was that he accused us of climbing White Needle Peak without his permission, when again we had discussed it with him and he had given us his verbal approval. We had a permission to climb Nun by its East Ridge and White Needle was actually a bump on the ridge. White Needle had to be crossed on the way to Nun. So when we returned to Srinagar at the end of the expedition the Director of Tourism at first asked us some direct questions about Neelam before the truth emerged.

Upon returning to England I wrote a long and detailed letter to the IMF complaining about Neelam and his behaviour. After some time the money was refunded and we asked Alok to pass the whole amount to Gafoor on our behalf. Many years later I was sitting in a hotel in Leh when I spotted Neelam at the check-in desk. We chose a quiet corner and he opened his heart out to me. He apologised for all his actions and told me he had never regretted anything more in his life. I discovered that when I had complained to the IMF they had taken the matter up with his employers who had then sacked him. He had almost lost his marriage, and strained his relations on both sides of his family. He said that he was grateful to me in a way, in that it had forced him to face up to the truth and make amends. He had saved to repay the debts and had started a new career which was going well he said, as a travel agent. It was an extraordinary meeting; I have never received such a complete and sincere apology in my life, before or since.

Back at Base Camp, shortly after Neelam left, finally the blissful sunshine we had enjoyed so far turned to militant clouds and soon a storm broke. We had managed a few days' climbing and had established an Advance Base Camp at 18,400ft/5,608 metres but the weather looked increasingly threatening. It started to snow and for four days and five nights we were trapped. We had a large circular mess tent of a new strengthened design and all day every day we played Scrabble, read books, slept, wrote diaries, cooked food and brewed endless cups of tea. Playing 'Solo' had an added interest as Norman Croucher had brought with him two sets of cards with naked girls on the backs. Norman was our Drinks Officer and had only joined the expedition at a late stage. Already he was a legend in the villages that we had passed through. Word travelled ahead of us, and whenever we approached a village the children would come out to see the strange man with no legs. He would let them approach and taking his ice axe he would swing down and strike his artificial legs a resounding blow. The kids were awestruck, and usually ran off in fright.

It was ironic Norman was the Drinks Officer as it had been drink that had been his undoing. As a young man he had fallen down drunk on a railway line and a train had severed both legs below the knee. The first thing he did upon leaving hospital on his new legs was to walk from John O'Groats to Land's End. After that he had climbed more peaks in the Alps than the rest of us put together, successfully climbed twenty thousand foot peaks in the Andes, and raised lots of money for disabled charities. Always in good humour, always laughing Norman had learnt to make jokes about himself and his disability. He also often jokingly said that at least he didn't have the problem of getting frostbite. Any wild scheme in the air and there was Norman at the heart of it. Could we trust him with the drink though?

The temperatures plummeted, the wind howled and several feet of snow fell. It made movement, particularly bowel movement, highly unpleasant. At regular intervals we ventured outside to dig out the tents. Meals were cooked underground as we had dug a snow trench kitchen and given it a roof. Sleeping was punctuated by dreams of being buried alive.

Then the sun shone and we strapped on heavy sacks for a carry to Advance Base Camp. Although we had snow shoes and mountaineering skis it was agonising work under a sweltering sun through deep snow.

Advance Base Camp. Mt Nun on the left, White Needle to the right.

We took it in turns to break trail at the front; stamping the snow down until it was compact enough to stand up on then repeating the process, hour after hour after hour, fifteen or twenty steps at a time. The enforced stay at Base Camp though had gained us valuable acclimatisation, but we were anxious not to lose any more time. That very same night back at Base it snowed again covering our tracks and the whole process had to be repeated. Halfway to ABC there was a level spot where we invariably stopped for a rest, and where rucksacks that had been over-ambitiously filled were lightened. This dump of food and gear grew as the build up to ABC proceeded and mountain choughs attacked our expedition boxes to get at the food inside.

At the very end of the expedition, when we were clearing the camps, I was on my own on my way to ABC and arriving at the dump, several hours from the nearest camp, I was shocked to find the expedition boxes scattered over a wide area. They had been attacked by a bear. We had been past the dump only the previous afternoon and everything was alright then. The bear prints in the snow were clearly fresh, and I anxiously looked around me. My axe was my only means of defence and I found myself gripping it with both hands half expecting the hungry bear to return. Our kit had been packed into boxes and the creature had just taken swipes at them, smashing everything. A thick metal cooking pot lay in the snow with four holes in its side. It must have been packed inside a box and the bear's claws went through the box and the metal pot. I carried on up to ABC feeling very vulnerable.

The route to Camp 1 also presented us with no climbing difficulties, just two large crevasses to avoid. However, it was easy to get lost on this section if the cloud moved in, and we marked the route with flagged bamboo canes. The site for the tents was on a small shelf on the very edge of a vertical precipice at the height of 19,500ft/5,944 metres. It lay at the foot of the ridge that now led up towards White Needle Peak. It must have been somewhere near here that the Old Man had stopped Tom Stobart from falling to his death. The panorama of peaks had now really opened up for us. To the south, east and west was a vast array of amazing Himalayan peaks. To the south east stood the pristine, frightening North Face of Zanskar 1, and beyond could be picked out Sickle Moon, Bramah 1 and literally hundreds more, most of them unnamed, unclimbed and not even surveyed. Nun still towered above us, blocking our view of the Karakoram, but now we could see the route ahead. It looked steeper and more dangerous than we had imagined from the photographs we had.

Bad weather moved in again pinning down my brother Richard and Barry Needle at Camp 1. Barry had of course been one of the strongest climbers on the East Toss expedition. Norman, myself and John Margesson sat it out at ABC while Steve Monks and Damian Caroll were enjoying a rest at Base. A day spent lolling around in a tent seems to pass by all too quickly. A lot of time is taken up with thinking about, discussing, preparing and eating food. At high altitude wild cravings develop for ham sandwiches, sausages, steak and chips, mushrooms on toast, bacon and eggs, and fish and chips. Only real ale and cheese is missed more. We kept consciously estimating our stock of food which was dwindling all too quickly. However, things did gradually improve and between bouts of bad weather we managed another two carries to Camp 1, Richard and Barry climbed halfway up White Needle, and Steve and 'Damo' came up again from Base with another surprise visitor.

Robin Moyors was a freelance journalist, a Vietnam veteran who had washed up in India somehow, and who, hearing that there was an expedition to Nun which included a man without legs, had also decided to chase on after us. He arrived with minimal gear at 19,500ft carrying half a box of cherries which he gave to us as a peace offering for disturbing our climb. Needless to say we ate the lot and regretted it shortly afterwards. He told us of fresh bear tracks all around our Base Camp, but luckily the bear had so far done no damage. He interviewed Norman for *Time Life* magazine, and after recounting wild tales of the American war machine long into the night fled with his porter the next day.

The quantities of snow that were falling upon us were appalling and one morning at ABC it completely covered the doorway making it difficult to get out. Temperatures most nights were -20°C and one night we recorded -30°C. Everything is such an effort at altitude. It's warm in your sleeping bag and it's -20°C outside, but when the snow is frozen solid it's a fraction of the effort to climb and three times as fast, and while the white stuff is frozen solid it is less likely to fall on your head. You have to get up. Hands and feet go numb, you knock things over, you curse freely, you are out of breath just doing up the boot laces. The list of 'hardships' is endless and it is easy to get out of proportion; to make it sound as though you are either a hero or an idiot to be there in the first place. The hardships are easily outweighed by the good times, especially in retrospect. The freedom, the beauty and power of Mother Nature, the great times with a bunch of friends, the heart pumping rush of fear under vague control, the recapturing of childish excitement, and for some people, the dream of becoming famous. We were a happy gang, and the Glorious Twelfth scotch was the next best thing to laughing gas. Unfortunately we had to leave it behind at Base Camp.

The weather improved slightly and as it turned out gave Norman and John Margesson the first crack at White Needle. If you met Norman in the street it would not be immediately obvious that he has artificial legs. He walks quickly and easily, and on the trek into Base Camp we had seen that he was only marginally slower than the rest of us. It was the same on snow; Norman was slightly slower but with his vast reserves of determination he had managed the diabolically exhausting carries. Looking ahead though I think we were all worried about whether he would be capable of climbing the steep ice slopes yet to come. In fact Norman was realistic about his chances of success. Only one out of the five previous expeditions to attempt Nun's East Ridge had succeeded and then only two of their fourteen Japanese climbers had achieved the summit. Norman's prime goals were to summit White Needle and thereby achieve an altitude record for a disabled climber. If a chance for the summit happened that would merely be a bonus.

On 11th June, John and Norman started from Camp 1 and we glimpsed them briefly going up the ridge before cloud moved in. At three o'clock they had reached 20,500ft/6,248 metres and with moderate wind and light snow they decided to stop and bivouac for the night. They dug a trench in the snow and slept in it in their Gore-Tex bivvy bags. The night was cold and stormy, and the next morning it was

Roy Berry on the summit of White Needle Peak, 1946. Hitting his feet with Spencer Chapman's ice axe to restore circulation. *Photo: Roy Berry Archive*

so cold that Norman only managed to get the cooker working by lighting it inside his rucksack. The weather was still poor and they waited until 9.00 a.m. before deciding to give it a try. Within five minutes John had gone thigh deep in a crevasse, something that happened to them several times during the day but luckily nothing worse than that. The bad weather had meant terrible snow conditions and John broke trail almost all the way, sinking up to his knees with each step. At one point they almost turned round as the weather closed in again, but with a few breaks in the cloud they carried on. Approaching the summit of White Needle the angle increased to fifty degrees and still they had to plough through deep snow. Then they hit the summit ridge running at right angles to their path up White Needle's steep back. They turned left keeping below the huge cornices with awful exposure on both sides. They reached the summit at 2.20 p.m. Through breaks in the cloud they could see that a col lay below, a fine campsite for Camp 2, and beyond lay the main difficulties of the east ridge. Norman had made his summit.

CHAPTER 5

Politics and the Climb of Nun

By now STEVE, DAMO, BARRY, RICHARD AND MYSELF were poised at Camp 1 to push the route on to Camp 2. We had begun to believe that the weather was never going to clear and the summit would never get any closer, but now on the 13th, the day after the 'Glorious Twelfth', the weather turned and the sun shone down out of a cloudless sky. Four of us clawed our way up the ridge, almost knife-edged in places with enormous drops either side, while Richard had a rest at Camp 1. Then, just after a steep section where we had put a fixed rope, Barry, in front of me, slipped on a section of ice. We had all become a bit too blasé about not bothering with crampons. He fell and stopped himself by using the point of his ski stick. For one horrible moment I thought he was going over the edge but he managed to get his axe free and recovered himself. I hastily put my crampons on!

We reached an area where the ridge broadened out into a small plateau before the final slopes of White Needle. From here we looked down on the enormous circular snow plateau, three miles wide, that lay between Nun and Kun. We were now almost level with the top of Zanskar 1. I did not climb White Needle that day as stupidly I had gone up in fairly minimal clothing and got very cold. I turned back but Steve, Damo and Barry carried on to the summit where Barry split his load between the other two. They dropped down to the saddle, pitched Camp 2 and were now all set for a rest, then a summit bid. Barry rejoined the rest of us now queuing up for our turn.

All through the trip we had enjoyed each other's company and it was only on the day Steve and Damo summited Nun that any 'politics' broke the surface. Richard and I had been watching the final climb through binoculars on our own rest day at Camp 1 when Norman arrived with a load. Norman was his usual self; the same jocular, hard bitten man of the mountains, but clearly was bottling something up. The upshot was that he had been sharing a tent with John for a week and couldn't stand his company any longer. John was too 'straight' for the party animal that lurked inside Norman. He'd had enough. He wanted to come with Richard and I to Camp 2 and wait for the others there. We pointed out that as he had come with a load it meant that we would be forced to wait one or two days while he went back to collect what he needed for the climb. He was adamant that he didn't want to hold Barry back, whom he held in deep respect. He thought John might drop out anyway because John had a desperately sore throat. He wanted to be up there to have a go if the conditions and the route allowed, and he didn't want to share a tent with John anymore. It was clear he couldn't join us, after all this is what it was all about for Richard and I – finishing the job off for the Old Man – and we couldn't wait for Norman. Norman accepted this with resignation.

Norm departed to go back to ABC, and half an hour later John arrived. We were then entertained to a similar little confessional from him. His gripe though was more serious. He was just not keen on Norman attempting Nun. In calm tones of quintessential English tact-fulness John said that although their ascent of White Needle had given him 'absolute respect for the man' he pointed to Norman's slowness and the length of the route. I tended to agree with him. We had watched Steve and Damo that very day take fifteen hours from a bivouac to the summit and back to the bergschrund bivvy, and they were our most accomplished, fittest climbers. I was worried Norman could endanger Barry and John. Right here was the most difficult decision of the trip, but I was not ready yet to stop Norman's attempt. Instead I swore John to secrecy and told him that he could use my veto as an absolute last resort to stop Norman *if* they reached Camp 2, *only if* Norman wanted to continue, *and then only if* he and Barry had come to the conclusion he was too slow. All three of us felt in any case that Norman would himself drop out if a situation arose where he was holding the other two up. We also all thought that because he had been so keen to do White Needle and had achieved it, Norman might well call it a day after supporting the other two to Camp 2. After John left, I started to worry whether morally I had done the right thing in giving John a powerful tool for him to misuse against Norman. I need not have worried.

This little cameo of behind the scenes wrangling was just a side show to the fact that after nearly a month of intense pain and patience we had succeeded. After two and a half years of raising money, planning and organising we had actually managed the summit. The over-riding atmosphere was actually of incredulous pride and a desire to get up there ourselves before the weather changed again. Summit day was the 16th, Barry and I had by this time already had an epic day trying to traverse across White Needle, across avalanche prone slopes, and failed while Richard had soloed White Needle. On the 15th he and I had left Camp 1, climbed White Needle, carried a load to Camp 2 and in a state of near exhaustion and collapse had staggered back down to Camp 1 for another rest.

Young bodies recover quickly. After climbing White Needle and dropping the loads at Camp 2 I had been shepherded down to Camp 1 by my brother, suffering giddy spells and a crashing headache, but a day drinking tea had turned my urine back from dark brown to clear. Porridge, dehydrated food and chocolate did the rest. We spent the day reading, discussing what mum and dad should have been doing with the family's small Trust, and periodically watching Steve and Damo's progress.

The day before we had also snatched glimpses of them, and had expected our star climbers to climb over some rock pinnacles that form the start of the East Ridge proper. We had seen them get to the base of the rocks and they had started to descend. We were puzzled and dis-appointed imagining that they were giving up, but to our surprise they then dropped below the ridge and began a long traverse many hundreds of feet below the East Ridge. In fact they kept just below the bergschrund formed at the base of Nun's steep avalanche prone South Face. We thought we could spot six avalanche tracks, but now we had had many days of thaw, freeze, thaw and avalanche activity on all the mountains around us had virtually stopped. We persuaded ourselves that now it would be safe enough. By 3.30 p.m. on the 15th Steve and Damo had parked themselves on the lip of the bergschrund, safe from avalanches, six or seven hundred feet below the ridge above.

On their summit day we watched them leave the bergschrund bivvy and could hardly believe it as it then took them four and a half hours just to complete the five pitches to gain the ridge. We kept thinking something was wrong, and then they disappeared from sight.

On the 17th Richard and I shouldered our heavy rucksacks and set off for Camp 2. It was Richard's turn to feel 'all-in' that day and we dumped some things from his sack on the way over White Needle. He picked up a bit. There at Camp 2 were the wide sunburnt grins of Steve and Damo. Too exhausted to do much more than hug them and ask about the route we took over the tent and waved them goodbye, as they made good use of our footsteps up and over White Needle. Just our luck though that night a small storm obliterated their tracks which we had hoped would save us time and energy. Nothing comes easy.

CHAPTER 6

Finishing the job

THE ALARM WENT AT 5.00 A.M. and Richard, always the mechanical genius, tinkered with the obstinate cooker, which was as reluctant as we were to get started. In the confined space of our two-man tent I managed to knock over one lot of snow melt water before leaving 'Tich' to cook the porridge breakfast while I went out into the mist to fix a snow stake anchor for us to abseil off the saddle.

When we were all set I abseiled first, only to find I had dropped over the edge in slightly the wrong place. The rope did not quite reach below the bergschrund and I was left dangling on the ice above. I drove in a couple of ice pegs and hung on them while Tich pulled up the rope and abseiled twenty yards to my left. Once he was safe below the bergschrund he threw me the rope and I lowered off to join him. The air was still, a few snow flakes fluttered down, but a few doubts about the weather were not enough justification for turning round.

Then started a horrible day of traversing across steep, rotten snow fields, mostly in mist, with snow up to our thighs in places. What we had hoped would take just a few hours took ten. I didn't think to count how many avalanche trails we clambered over. Some were old, some were fresh. We swore, we cried, we floundered and all the time up above millions of tons of snow and ice warmed in intermittent sunshine. To begin with we only broke through the snow's crust to calf height. Ten steps or fifteen, stop, lungs and heart at full throttle, rest, another ten or fifteen, collapse onto the head of your axe gasping, and so it went on not knowing how far we had come and how far it was to go. There were places where the snow was so deep and soft that progress almost stopped. One of these times I was all in favour of dumping the BBC's camera and its film. Richard offered to take it and as I wasn't having that, we dumped an axe instead. Every last ounce of weight means so much when you are struggling at your limits. Seeing the bergschrund bivvy that Steve and Damo had used prior to their summit day through a break in the clouds was such an utter relief. Even so the final slope to the ice shelf was brutal.

Tucked right in underneath a huge overhang of ice we at last knew we were safe. In our tiredness every little thing was a vast effort, but Tich somehow managed to coax the cooker to life and we enjoyed freeze dried sweet and sour pork, mixed up with mash, and tea. We banged in a couple of rock pegs into the wall at the back of our 'cave' and tied ourselves on. We were not sure what our ice shelf consisted of, and every now and then there were ominous cracks and the tinkle of chunks of ice falling down the wide gap we could see that was formed between the rock wall and the ice shelf. In pitch darkness, with the aid of our headtorches, we fought our way into our down sleeping bags, inside our double Gore-Tex bivvy bag and tried to sleep for a few hours.

The alarm went at 2.00 a.m. and I could just make out a few clouds going past. I woke Richard who worked his trick in the dark with the cooker and by 4.30 a.m. we were standing at the foot of the 650ft/200 metre slope wondering how the hell we were going to get over the bergschrund.

My younger brother and I had always been competitive. Maybe we were too competitive, and as kids I feel sure he suffered as a result. Still, by the time we were in our late teens, early twenties, we frequently went rock-climbing together and that is when finally we started to compete as equals. Blond haired, and still my mischievous brother, he was now as tall as and as strong me. Then in my mid-twenties I suffered a serious fall. I broke my nose, jaw, cheekbone, knee, and lost my sight in one eye for a couple of weeks. I didn't lose my love of climbing, but after that I was a lot more cautious and Richard usually took the lead.

So it was then that the first pitch was down to him. Trouble was though that even at its narrowest point the lip of the bergschrund reached down only to head height. We just couldn't get onto the ice above. The only way was for me to kneel down and for Richard to climb onto my shoulders. I stood up with great difficulty suffering at the same time the pain of his cramponed boots digging into my shoulders. Then he was up on the bare ice above. It was very cold as I stood paying out the rope, as ice chips showered down. Dawn approached as God turned up the dimmer switch on a bloodshot horizon. An hour and a half passed before Tich reached the single ice screw at ninety feet that constituted the belay. Hanging from this was Steve and Damo's abseil rope.

Then it was me to follow. I tried all sorts of things to get up onto the ice lip, and failed. Gasping, frustrated and angry this eventually turned into a blazing row as Tich became more and more impatient and time was sliding by. We had to climb the six hundred and fifty foot slope before the sun turned the hard packed snow above to mush. Finally, he tied some knots in Steve and Damo's rope and somehow I hauled myself onto the ice. I stood there wobbling on my front points, completely spent. This one pitch was the crux of the whole expedition. It was seventy degrees hard ice and at 22,000ft you just cannot go quickly. Bang in the front points, wham in the two axes, pull up. Calf muscles on fire, adrenalin at an all time high, forget about the ever increasing drop. Calm the panic monster threatening to break loose, and climb, and keep on climbing. Tich, like a benevolent God, slowly drew closer, standing nonchalantly on his chipped out footsteps, grinning the purest grin, his pre-war style goggles unforgettable.

After that one pitch the angle eased to sixty degrees and instead of bare ice it was overlaid with hard frozen snow. We switched leads and now the toes of my boots bit into the surface, and the axes sunk in with one easy blow. The inexorable wheels of the universe turned and the sun in no particular hurry lit the slow burning fuse on the slope above. No matter, at those altitudes the snow deteriorated less quickly. After each rope length we would kick out a 'bucket' to belay from and bang the axes into the hard snow as some sort of psychological anchor. It took us five and a half hours to reach a sensational knife-edged ridge that marked the top of the South Face.

By this time I really felt like a zombie, and dumped anything I thought inessential – some batteries, some spare film – nothing that really made any difference. From here the East Ridge rose up. At first it was knife-edged, and then broad and steeper for about five or six hundred feet, leading to a broad, almost flat area. The climb up to the broad flat area took hours and hours. Every step was a punishment, just plain cruel agony. I was frightened that my exhaustion and our horribly slow pace was going to endanger our lives. I was so tired that even the simplest of actions I was almost incapable of, like organizing the belaying. Richard did a lot of small things for me, whilst I whittered and complained. I really never thought we would make it, but of course it had to be done. I had failed at school, I had failed to enter Hamble to train as a pilot, I had been arrested at the age of nineteen for possession of cannabis, I had been kicked out of my dad's best friend's engineering company, and I had smashed up my mother's car on more than one occasion. At the root of it all was a hate, love relationship with the Old Man, more hate than love in fact. Now I was going to show him. Now he would see Richard and I were made of more than he gave us credit for.

By now it was as much as I could do to lift one foot in front of the other, there was no case of competing with Tich. I didn't even have brain power to count each set of steps; five or seven at a time I think. In any case I was not into trying to beat him. We were brothers, we would do it together.

For every step I was also aware of the yawning drops on either side and that the sea of snow giants in every direction was slowly but surely falling below me. I was struggling along in a place of incomparable beauty. Since the first few clouds at 2.00 a.m. it had cleared completely, and as the day wore on a sea of cloud gradually built up in every direction as far as the eye could see. Virtually all the distant ranges became clogged with cloud, only our mountain and its satellites basked in sunshine. Someone, something seemed to be laying it on for us.

Shortly after the saddle I was so buggered that again I wanted to drop the BBC camera, and would have done, had not Richard forcibly volunteered to carry it. Instead this time we left the aluminum 'Deadman' snow anchor, and on we slowly went. Richard always seemed to be sitting on a stance above me looking calm, unperturbed, stoic with the occasional grin, cajoling me on, with the brolly still strapped to the back of his sack. We were going to leave it on the summit as an expression of the mad English. Beside someone on the summit might find it useful, if it was snowing for instance!

Existence was total agony, punctuated by rests at the stances contemplating the worse agony to come, and watching in awe the mountain world. There was ever the slope above, and a stubborn person inside of me trying to retain some interest in getting there. The only reward would have been to rest. Richard promised me rests to keep me going, and somewhere I knew I was going to make it, and I could still just about laugh inside. At the broad area we stopped to eat a Mars bar and drink some mixture of Staminade and Rise and Shine. I wanted so much to sleep. The summit still looked miles away, but at least we could see it now. Tich stopped to load a black and white film, so I went on slowly, a ragged piece of human jetsam stumbling along. Now we could see Steve and Damo's steps, one minute on the north side of the mountain, then the south. All was stillness and freezing cold, and now there were a few rocks poking up through the snow. First a false summit and then it was almost flat. Steve and Damo's steps stopped one hundred feet from the summit but literally only a few feet lower. There had been cloud and they genuinely thought they were on the summit; to all intents and purposes they had been.

Just before we got to the summit I stopped and said, "Go on, you go first, you've done all the work today. You deserve it." Then we were hugging each other next to the small wooden cross, shaking hands and laughing.

We were conscious of the time, 5.00 p.m., time enough to set up a remote release piece of film with Tich pretending to be blown away by the brolly. We took panorama photos, and had only a few minutes to gaze out over a sea of cloud. There were thoughts of Dr. Mutch's body said to be near the summit, of dad's pride at our succeeding, and of the dangerous descent ahead. Then we were off. Easy, easy, easy until we got to the knife-edge ridge and the start of the six hundred and fifty feet slope back to the bivvy. Looking down that slope was a time when I knew fear. We both knew that if one of us slipped and fell that the belays would probably rip out. There just could not be any mistakes. It was not as bad as we had feared. It was still possible to kick into the slope even though the snow was softer. The problem was more one of tiredness. I was so dead beat that, well, if we came off and died so what. Fear disappeared and the endurance test went beyond its climax. Like a rambling mantra I talked to myself, repeating over and over that I must concentrate on every step, mustn't let the concentration wane. Then we were abseiling off the single ice screw down the ice pitch and in a flurry of ice we shot over the bergschrund and were safe, at least for the time being.

I was in a crazed condition, hardly aware of what was happening. I knew it was getting cold and dark and that I was hungry and thirsty, but what I needed was sleep and warmth. Somehow I got into my sleeping bag and there were vague sensations of Tich doing something, kneeling on my head by mistake, then being choked by spindrift, the bivvy bag being zipped and sleep came on strong, oblivion.

CHAPTER 7

The Austrian Chiefs, and the Avalanche

WE AWOKE AT 7.00 A.M. as the sun hit the shambles that was our bivvy. It had snowed in the night, the wind had blown it in and now everything was covered, but who cares when you are dead to the world. Combine fierce heat, altitude, lack of food and extreme tiredness and it is easy to imagine reaching a state where you would never move, but just die. My aunt Madge in her mid eighties said to me once, "Steven, it is so hard to die." I am sure she was right, but we were not about to find out on that day. The grumpy stove heated porridge for two grumpy men, and fours hours later we left, leaving the cooker, food, bivvy bag and climbing equipment hanging on an ice peg for John, Norman and Barry. We were very weak and even going downhill meant frequent rests. Out of the mist appeared three figures. So the trump card had not been played. The proud summit team imparted its wisdom. The aspirants listened attentively, but there was no time to hang around. We had to get out of the avalanche danger and so a few hours later we were at the fixed rope hanging down from the saddle. There was so little strength left that we both had 'rubber' legs, and the thought of climbing the steep one hundred and fifty feet to the saddle was worrying. This was the scene for a blazing row between two stubborn mules. I favoured leading the pitch without a rucksack and then hauling one sack at a time to save energy, but Tich couldn't be bothered with this. In the end we did it his way and perhaps it was the row that injected enough adrenalin to pump us up the slope. We were safe at Camp 2!

There were reserves to draw on yet, and a rest and a drink was enough for us to contemplate the climb back over White Needle. In fact whether it was the drop in altitude, or the gathering joy at knowing for us the job was done, or more likely both, we did find power and purpose again. Not content to stop at Camp 1 we then carried on down arriving totally spent at Advance Base at 7.00 p.m. Steve and Damo welcomed us in with a very hot curry and gallons to drink. We celebrated being alive and talked about our trials till two in the morning. So happy now that I sang and shouted into the night.

The next three days were cloudy and we dossed around. We read, played Scrabble and solo whist, cooked and ate, filmed an intelligent mountain chough angling for food, listened to music and I wrote my diary. Before long the worry began for the other three, but on the evening of the second day the cloud cleared briefly and we thought we saw two sets of tracks on the six hundred and fifty foot slope. They must have gone up and down. On the third day we saw them descending towards Camp 1 and half expected them to come down to Advance, but it wasn't until midday on the fourth day that they appeared. Barry and John had climbed Nun, and Norman had unselfishly elected to stay at the bivvy in the bergschrund. The ice pitch had been too much and he had worried that even if he had somehow got up onto the ice, that he would have perhaps ruined the chances of the others making the top. Nevertheless 22,000ft was a world record altitude at that time for a disabled climber.

That day we set about packing up and heading for Base Camp. None of us had been there for nineteen days and we were keenly looking forward to the whisky and chocolate stored in the mess tent. The Drinks Officer was intent on fulfilling his duties!

Firstly we constructed two sledges by lashing our two sets of cross-country skis to a couple of solid pack frames. Two people towed the sledges, while everyone else hauled loads in heavy duty plastic bags. We all carried far too much in our rucksacks, and off we went. Laughably on anything of a slope the sledges took off and were brutes to stop. On one steep slope we just cut them loose and roared with laughter as they hurtled down and crashed at the bottom. How the bottom of the mountain had changed! During our three weeks at 18,000ft/5,500 metres and above a huge melt had taken place. Ridges that were snow-covered were now bare rock, crevasses had opened up, pools and streams had appeared.

Base Camp hove into sight but the next grand surprise was that we had been raided, but not by the bear! We entered the circular mess tent and were shocked to find that our neatly organized supplies and our bags of personal kit had been strewn around the floor. The locked tent had been broken into and ransacked. A huge quantity of things had been stolen, including the whisky, money, clothing, food, passports and air tickets. One moment there was the welcome sight of Base and the prospect of a real celebration, and the next anger, confusion and disappointment.

As we were making an inventory someone noticed a climber going downhill some distance from our abused Base. Damo went after him and followed the man to another Base Camp about half an hour away. He came back with half a bottle of whisky and a strange explanation. They were an Austrian expedition attempting Nun's sister peak Kun. They had been told by the IMF there was no one else on the mountain, had heard about the helicopter evacuation, and as there was no sign of anyone around, they had entered the tent and found Monksie's diary with the last entry 23rd May. It was now 24th June. They had concluded that we had abandoned our camp and had descended via another valley.

We were seething, and Norman was all for starting World War III and going down and attacking their camp! Their logic was absolutely ridiculous of course; who would leave passports, air tickets, money and a fully stocked camp! Maybe they thought we had all perished in an avalanche. Anyway the debate raged into the evening and whatever they thought had happened to us it was wrong to have stolen our food, spilt our kerosene, made off with our climbing hardware, purloined our unused film, and turned all our tents upside down. Their leader, Damo had been told, was going to come up the following morning to explain, and I was voted the job of interviewing him.

The next morning dawned bright and clear and after a while Franz Holnzenburger entered our camp and was shown into the mess tent. The others left and I sat down placing a tape recorder between us and hit the record button. I guess he was in his fifties and spoke in amusing Pidgin English. He was a worried man! I pointed out that we had every right to report the matter to the Indian police, the IMF, the Austrian Alpine Club, the Himalayan Club, and to publish the facts in the international press, the Austrian press and the mountaineering magazines. He begged me to believe that they were not 'chiefs' which he kept repeating. It took me a while to realize that 'chiefs' meant thieves. He said he would do anything they could to make compensation. Now was the time to strike! I extracted monetary compensation, a promise to return our belongings, paraffin and a gas stove that we needed for our attempt on Zanskar 1 (our secondary objective), tinned food and some of their incredibly tasty smoked sausages. What I was not expecting was an offer from him to take Norman with them on their ascent of Kun. They had heard all about Norman and now his disappointment at not succeeding on Nun, and had obviously thought this was the way to claw back a little of the moral high ground. Franz did point out they would have to have their Liaison Officer's approval, but we thought in the circumstances this should be a formality. We did in fact part on friendly terms, and after he was out of earshot there was a lot of laughter at his expense. Days later we did get back what remained of our whisky, though they had drunk half of it, our money, passports, airline tickets, and half the chocolate.

Now our focus moved to the possible lightweight attempt on Zanskar 1. Steve and Damo voted against it saying they thought the route looked too dangerous. Instead they started the business of dismantling the camps and moving gear down the mountain. The rest of us packed four days' food and set off the next day. Norman generously offered to carry a load for us to the foot of the climbing proper, and was lucky enough to see, close to, a herd of Ibex on his way back to camp. By midday we had crossed under the easy slopes of Zanskar 1's subsidiary peak, and had climbed some easy ice slopes to a sloping snowfield. This lay several hundred feet below a set of more serious ice cliffs. We unroped and sat down to have some lunch and after a few minutes heard a thunderous rumble. Tich said, "That's a big one" and I replied, "Yeah, but it's not here though." In an instant the thunderous rumble became a deafening roar and we jerked round to see the avalanche pouring over the cliffs above us. John shouted "Run!" Instantly I was up and running down the slope. I remember heart bursting, lungs pumping, and a sickening knowledge that this was it, I stood no chance. I tripped over my crampons and fell face down in the snow, and expected to be flattened any second. I got up, ran again, and someone shouted, "This way Steve."

Avalanche on Zanskar 1 that nearly killed us.

I could see figures off to my left. I swerved and saw chunks of ice flying by. I reached the others and swung round to see what was happening. The avalanche swept past us literally yards away and in that same instant someone was being thrown into the air and then engulfed. I screamed, "No, not Richard," but it wasn't my brother, it was Barry. As we watched the whole thing came to a halt and Barry was there struggling upright, and limping towards us. In the immediate aftermath we suffered from shock, and stood dazed, not quite sure what to do. Tich moved back to where we had been eating lunch and started finding things. He pulled a rope out, found a rucksack. We only lost three ice screws and a ski stick. If we hadn't unclipped from the rope we would never have got out the way in time, and if it had been ten minutes later I would have been leading up the ice. Tich said, "That's our warning, let's count ourselves lucky and go down." Needless to say we all agreed, and in any case Barry had a badly bruised leg and needed helping back to camp.

On the way back Barry and I came to a foaming stream, with a snow bridge. It was only about four feet wide and I went across first. At the other side I put my sack down and as I turned round, the snow bridge collapsed into the stream. It took us ages to walk back upstream until we came to another larger snow bridge that Barry could cross. At the Austrians' camp that evening we were made very welcome by two of their team. They cooked us some meat in a sauce with ravioli strips, followed by tinned cherries, Austrian cheese, German bread with coffee and slices of smoked bacon and mustard. We had lived to tell the tale.

CHAPTER 8

The Professor and the Kingdom of Zanskar

THERE WAS STILL PLENTY TO DO. Tich was going to carry out a survey and make a map, there were several carries needed to clear the remaining equipment from Advance, and there was still the question of Norman joining the Austrians.

Word had come down from their Camp 1 that the Liaison Officer had vetoed the idea, so not to be beaten Norman had climbed up to visit them to argue his case. He convinced the LO, but then there must have been some internal politics within their team and next thing we heard was that they had taken a vote, and the majority had voted 'no' to the idea. Norman understandably was by now less than enamoured of the entire Germanic race, and all of us were angry that after offering Norman a place in their first summit team, five days later they had reneged on their offer. We concluded that their leader was an idiot.

Work carried on, and this was the time when I came across the 'dump' which had been attacked by the bear. We had heard that the bear had recently been seen by one of the Austrians' porters, and that one evening it had been heard prowling around their mess tent. No doubt it could smell the smoked bacon and sausages, as we could. I have to admit that whenever there were no Austrians around a few slices were surreptitiously shaved off the meats hanging from a line in their mess tent. We felt they owed us. The bear came into our camp one night and I remember vividly lying stock still in my sleeping bag as its nose sniffed along the wall of our tent, inches from my face.

Barry's leg mended incredibly quickly and within two days he was carrying loads again, though his calf had gone luridly purple. One of the Austrians had seen the avalanche that had nearly killed us and had taken a photo. He promised to send us a copy, which he did many months later. The avalanche was a cornice that had broken off the summit ridge of the subsidiary peak. By the time we left, the Austrians had retreated to their Base on account of all the bad weather that Norman had wished upon them. The only other injuries we sustained were some minor frostbite to fingers and thumbs for John and Tich. The tips had gone white and feeling was lost for a while.

We dug a pit for any rubbish we could not burn and refrained from just tossing our garbage down crevasses. We covered the pit with heavy rocks and just hoped that the Ursus excavator would not dig it all up again. The first two horses and porters appeared at Moraine Camp and efficient John relished the responsibility of organizing the loads, while Tich and I planned to visit Ringdom gompa; the monastery that dad had chanced upon while hunting for food at the end of his climb.

We had done more than our fair share of the work and the others were happy to finish bringing the kit to Gulamantongus, the camp next to the river crossing, on 6th July. That gave us four days.

When Tich and I reached the river again we found to our surprise that it had risen so much that there was no hope of wading across. We had not allowed for this in our planning. Luckily for us the Austrians had. On the other side of the river was a rather smart looking yellow rubber boat, guarded by two porters. A climbing rope was strung across the swift flowing river that they could use to pull themselves across by. We naturally assumed they would come across and pick us up, but they would not. We shouted, we gesticulated, we wrapped messages round rocks and threw them across, and after an hour and a half of this we simply got as mad as hell. Eventually they did come across and reaching our bank we greeted each other like long lost relatives. A few rupees passed hands.

We then walked down the road a bit and found a place to put up the tent. It was hot, hot, hot and we barely had energy to do anything. We had heard that lorries taking goods to the small capital township of the Kingdom of Zanskar, Padum, passed this way infrequently. We half expected to have to wait for a day or two, but several hours later we could see two trucks heading our way from Kargil. We thought it might be a Spanish expedition that was due to arrive on 1st July but incredibly it was our friend Ghulam Rasool and the five porters we had ordered. Also sitting on top of one of the trucks was an English professor and five of his students on their way to study the mating habits of yaks in Zanskar. The really astonishing thing was that they were from Bristol University. We were the first British team to come to the mountain for thirty five years, since my father in 1946, and yet within two or three hours of reaching the roadhead there appeared Dr. Henry Osmaston, a quintessential absent-minded professor from our own home town. The coincidence seemed remarkable. Nor was Henry just any person passing by, but it was not until many years later that I discovered that Henry was a founding member of the International Institute for Ladakh Studies. It was his introduction in 1987 to the King of Padum that led me later to understand that there was a strange connection between the ancient kingdoms of Ladakh and Bhutan.

The connection is that the most powerful king of Ladakh, Senge Namgyal (1570–1640), and the first ruler of Bhutan, Nawang Namgyal (whose title became the 'Shabdrung' 1594–1651) had formed an alliance against the most powerful Dalai Lama of Tibet, the Great 'Fifth' (1617–1682) who was at that time threatening Ladakh. Senge and Nawang lived one thousand miles apart at either end of the Himalaya in the days before roads, and yet had somehow combined forces. Senge had given Nawang lands on which to build his Drukpa, or dragon people, monasteries. He had apparently invited him to be the head monk in Ladakh. Much of the detail of this story is surrounded in mystery, and perhaps the facts are long forgotten, I don't know. What I do know is that it is as intensely mystical as the Himalaya is itself. How is it that, for instance, Mount Kailash, in western Tibet, regarded by Buddhists, Hindus, Jains and Bonpos as the physical and spiritual centre of the universe, was 'gifted' to the Shabdrung? How is it that this extraordinary mountain, the repository of spiritual power in the eastern world, was in fact ringed by four Bhutanese monasteries? Right up until the Chinese invasion of Tibet there used to be a high Bhutanese personage living at the foot of Kailash acting as an administrator. The people who lived in Darchan, the small town at the foot of Kailash, regarded themselves as Bhutanese, and even the early kings of Bhutan exchanged letters with their governor who lived in a large house there. The strange connection with the king of Padum was that he himself was a direct descendant from the early kings of Tibet and was a follower of the Shabdrung. He had even built a temple and a house for him (the Shabdrung was then living in exile in Manali) on the hill that sits above Padum township, where his ancestors' castle used to stand. The castle was destroyed when the Kashmiris invaded in the early 1800s. Henry Osmaston and his close friend Dr. John Crook wrote several books about Zanskar, not just about the mating habits of yaks, but on every aspect of Zanskari life, history and culture. They were firm friends of Punchok Dawa, the king of Padum, and in meeting Henry I unwittingly set off a series of events in later life that would connect me too with Zanskar.

It was doubly lucky that Richard and I met Henry at the side of the road because we were able to beg a lift off his party to Padum. Also our

porters were too afraid to re-cross the swollen river in the boat. The two
rogues at the riverside told them the rope was unsafe, so Rasool decided
to carry on in the lorries as far as the Pensi La pass and drop his men off
there, where they could cross easily, and then they could walk back
down in two days to Gulamantongus, opposite the raft. How the hell
they were then going to cross the river with the rest of our expedition
and the gear we couldn't imagine. For Tich and I it was another two
hours in the trucks on a very bad road to Yuldo, the village that lies six
kilometres from Ringdom gompa. The lamasery sits on top of a hillock
that dominates a large, flat wide valley. A mystical land of people in
purple robes and head-dresses studded with turquoise, and mountains all
around. The trucks were going on to Padum the next day, a journey of
one hundred kilometres, so we decided to take the ride that was offered.

First though we had to visit Ringdom armed with dad's black and
white photos, to see if anyone there recognized any of the monks in his
pictures. Sadly the lamas we met did not. The medieval building itself
looked as though it had not changed one iota from those far off days. In fact
a patina of ancientness was imbued in everything there; the dung-caked
alley, the courtyards with chortens containing the ashes of long dead lamas,
the inner temples with their huge idols, even the monks performing a
morning ritual chanting from prayer books, the latter hundreds of years old.
There was the pungent smell of yak butter and incense, dust laden strips of
sunlight striking gruesome wall paintings, and we both remarked that one
of the monks himself looked at least one hundred and fifty years old.

Monks at Ringdom gompa in 1946. *Photo: Roy Berry Archive*

Then it was on to Padum. A long, tiring and dusty journey, passing through many Zanskari villages in which the houses were made of mud bricks and painted white, with flat roofs stacked with fodder and kindling. Past many unknown impressive peaks, as our tired truck zigzagged up countless hairpin bends, bucking and belching diesel fumes, over the 14,500ft Pensi La Pass. We had been stuffing our emaciated bodies with food at every opportunity and after the bone-shaking ride arrived at Padum with constipation. Zanskar has two kings; one of whom lives in the village of Zangla, and Punchok Dawa, who I have mentioned above, and who still lived in Padum. Tich and I were unaware of this at the time.

The intensity of what we had done, what we had achieved, what pain we had lived through, what luck we had received placed a certain and permanent smile on our faces. We were sightseers in a strange and far off land. We talked and laughed with the Muslim driver and the Ladakhis we met, we stayed up all hours soaking up their tough life, sharing their diabolically hot curry, drinking their rough alcohol, but all the time we were still up there above the clouds just struggling along.

The time came when we had to say goodbye to our friend the amiable professor, turn around and head back on the lorry to meet the others. It was not until many years later that the professor appeared again.

Our friends had packed up the last camp in a snowstorm, the Austrians had failed, the reluctant ferrymen had lent us the raft, and we were back to watching our possessions, haggling over every last rupee, and enduring sixteen-hour truck rides to reach the idyll of Srinagar. There we were given official receptions, presented with medals, interviewed by television, radio and Indian national newspapers, and there were promises of retribution against our Liaison Officer. We lived aboard fragrant cedar wood houseboats, and those of us who had them were met by their girlfriends and moved into swanky hotels. We rode in Shikaras across the mirror smooth lakes, lounging like lizards, watching the diving kingfishers, were beset by Kashmiri shop keepers, hashish peddlers, and we drooled longingly over the silk carpets, papier-mâché handicrafts and elaborately carved wooden furniture. Some of it found its way into the expedition kit and flew home with us when we finally had to tear ourselves away.

CHAPTER 9

Towards the Turquoise Mountain

I HAD TO WAIT TWO AND A HALF YEARS until the next big trip. The illnesses, the fact that on the mountain you don't bathe for a month, the cramped condition of living in a small tent shared with some other smelly, farting human for weeks on end, the bed bugs and flea bites, the bone-jarring road journeys and the myriad other 'hardships' are soon forgotten. The incurable romantic ruthlessly deletes them from memory. Flooding back come the daydreams of huge mysterious peaks, full of legend, verging on the inaccessible, in a land of mystical culture, full of exotic adventure. Back come the desires for comradeship and the pleasures of Sherpa hospitality. You start imagining yourself climbing ever upwards to that place where the horizon is gently curved, where there is nothing but a sea of peaks and cloud below you. You want the freedom to do as you please, the release from petty worldly cares, and you want to achieve.

Ambition settled on me, not for fame or fortune, just to climb something even bigger than Nun. Well if we could climb a 7,000 metre peak why not one of the fourteen 8,000 metre peaks. I started researching. At that time only a handful had been climbed by British parties. Eventually our gang of Bristol climbers settled on Cho Oyu, 26,906ft/8,201 metres, the sixth highest peak in the world, as our next big wheeze.

Who has ever heard of Cho Oyu? A few perhaps, but unlike most other 8,000ers it had been climbed only a handful of times and never, at that time, by the British. Books written about it numbered less, photos were rare, and as it had been 'off-limits' until the early 1980s, it had been rarely visited. It is remote, twenty miles north west of Everest, on the Nepalese/Tibetan border. It seemed never to have attracted much attention, and had hidden until then behind the back of Everest, safeguarded by the immovable face of Nepalese bureaucracy.

Its history is full of the unusual and the extraordinary, and often the truth of the stories is difficult to establish. The British did a lot of the early reconnaissance, including an attempt by Eric Shipton in 1952, which failed at 22,400ft. It was this failure so low on the mountain, and criticisms of his leadership, that led eventually to Shipton being supplanted as leader of the 1953 Everest expedition.

The first ascent was a very remarkable feat, accomplished without oxygen by an Austrian, Herbert Tichy, in 1954. Four European climbers made a daring push of nearly 4,000ft/1,200 metres from their last camp to the summit. Tichy had climbed back up from the foot of the mountain with badly frostbitten hands. Even more remarkable, his Sherpa, Ang Dawa Lama, came from his village of Marlung thirty miles away, and below 4,000 metres, to reach the summit with Tichy and Sepp Jöchler in an incredible three days. The magic of the mountain lured Dawa Lama back to the summit four years later with the second successful expedition from his native India.

The drama of Tichy's climb was enlivened by the appearance of another French/Swiss team, which was supposed to be on another mountain, Gauri Sankar, and which proceeded to compete for the honours on Cho Oyu. Frenchwoman, Claude Kogan, reached 24,700ft/7,529 metres, but her team quit the mountain in poor weather after Tichy's successful ascent. She too returned five years later with an all-female team and perished, as did three of her companions, in two avalanches. It was some coincidence that her previous success was the first ascent of Nun in 1953, seven years after my father's attempt. If we stood on the top, it would be the third highest peak ever climbed by the British, after Everest and Kangchenjunga – K2 was only climbed by a Brit in 1986, two years later.

After two years of painstaking organisation the Advance Party was in serious disarray! Harry missed the bus to Heathrow, Jeff lost his air ticket, and I lost my brolly. We found that our bottled oxygen, intended as medical back-up in Base Camp, should have gone through cargo and we only got it on board the plane by me signing an indemnity the consequence of which could have resulted in law suits totalling millions against my pitiful estate. In the airport there was a fantastic succession of scenes of chaos, punctuated by flashing camera bulbs, flapping airline officials, and the excited faces of my family. Even the Old Man was there looking tired and lonely. I realised, and not for the first time, that I would never know what went on inside him.

The previous evening had been a terrible, late booze up and I was still throwing things into bags at 3.00 a.m., thankfully not paper bags. People had been ringing me up all day wishing me luck, and there had been a party at the office from my more than tolerant employers. Poor old Jeff had to miss the flight, but Harry raced to the airport in his MGB sports car and made it in time. We were handed a case of Glorious Twelfth whisky by some gorgeous, lovely girl from the distillers in front of the cameras and off we went. After stops at Rome and Athens we landed at Bombay and the pilot hit the runway so hard he burst a bunch of hydraulic pipes in the undercarriage, and Biman Bangladesh Airlines carted their unhappy passengers off to a hotel by the sea. In the lobby I met Mary, an Irish girl, on her way to go travelling around Australia. It was one of those rare times when lust at first sight worked for two people. She was also stranded, and within an hour we were walking hand in hand along a beach beside the Indian Ocean. The heat, the rhythmic swish of the waves, the palm trees, the stranded fishing smacks that looked Arabian; it all felt so timeless. It was a surreal setting for our kissing and touching. There was no guilt; we both knew that tomorrow we would say goodbye. There was nowhere to go either to make love. Harry was in our room, Mary was sharing a room with another woman from the flight. We ended up like teenagers heavy petting in a hotel corridor.

At 2.00 a.m. we were woken and told we were going to the airport as there was a flight to Kathmandu for us via Calcutta and Dacca. Unfortunately for me, Mary was getting off in Calcutta. We spent a happy few hours at 30,000ft discussing all the things we would like to do to each other if only we had the chance. A fond farewell and Harry and I were on again to Dacca, capital of Bangladesh. We landed at 8.30 a.m. and were made to wait with no explanation until 1.30 p.m. when we were pushed from pillar to post, tired, hot and very pissed off with Biman Bangladesh Airlines, until it suddenly dawned on us that they had double-booked the flight up to Kathmandu and we were being taken to another hotel in Dacca.

We were stuck there for two days, so to keep fit Harry and I pedalled our own rickshaws, with the owners as laughing passengers, and raced each other around the back streets and bazaars much to the amusement of the general populace. We took ferry rides up the Ganges in boats that, with one big wave, would have sunk with all passengers. We poked around half empty museums, and met a motley selection of travellers. We met the unctuous millionaire Bangladeshi hotel owner, a pair of Italian doctors, and an American come to Dacca to install a space tracking station. We tried to avoid an Australian woman Helen who ran her own yoga centre in Indonesia and who was 'great friends with the Dalai Lama', a German who should have been wearing a steel helmet, and a woman who had lived in Athens for five years but who was now moving to Australia to become a professional tennis player. Then there was a German couple who we instantly distrusted who said they ran a removal business in Germany but who we thought were drug runners, and who spent all the time in their hotel room. There was a wide-eyed and frightened young boy who lived in London but who was coming to Dacca to visit his Bengali father, Sandy and Rachel, two American girls travelling the east for five months, and an assortment of extremely petty officials, smiling waiters learning the art of tip collecting, and at the bottom of the scale impoverished hustlers and beggars.

After all that when we were taken back to Dacca airport lo and behold there was the rest of the expedition, just arrived. We flew into Kathmandu together on some sort of Focker aircraft that the Germans seemed immensely proud of. In those days Kathmandu Airport was just a rather large, hot shed full of shouting gesticulating masses. We figured we had done well when the Customs Officers only impounded the walkie talkies, the oxygen and the whisky. We miraculously recovered the main expedition gear which had travelled ahead of Harry and I, and was lying in a heap in the corner of the shed amongst a massive pile of other boxes, bags and sacks of unclaimed baggage.

We jumped into four taxis for a fantastic ride through the usual jumble of decaying streets but it was easy to see why the hippies had made it their home. Not just because there was a seemingly inexhaustible supply of black hash, but because the ancientness of its temples and palaces made it feel like you were walking into a dream. Perhaps in a sense we were. Anyway Doug Scott, the first Englishman who returned from Everest with proof that he had been on the summit, had recommended a good hotel to us. The owner turned out to have been a Sherpa with Claude Kogan on her fateful expedition to Cho Oyu.

We spent a full week in Kathmandu, most of it in government offices, and one or two members passed the time by occasionally testing the black hash for quality control. I had never seen so many dingy offices, piled high with stacks of files that looked like they had sat on desks waiting for years for somebody to do something with them. I sat for hours in corridors and ante rooms, moving from one ministry to the next, form filling, paying bribes, paying Customs Duties, obtaining an Import Licence, varying the route on our climbing permit, being briefed by the Ministry of Tourism, meeting the Liason Officer, meeting Under

Secretaries, and trying to deal with a film permit, as the BBC were going to make another regional documentary. Every evening we held an expedition meeting in our hotel to discuss the best ways of getting out of Kathmandu as fast as we could. Costs were spiralling; we had decided to buy a lot more fixed rope and the taxes and backhanders had taken their toll. On the evening of the fourth day we had a crisis meeting. We went through the finances, again and again, and it was painfully obvious we were short of money. For me it was also a literally physically painful meeting as I had just come down with a virulent bug and had to go to the toilet every ten minutes. At one point sitting on the toilet I was puking and shitting at the same time. I felt as bad as it is possible to feel, fever, drenched in sweat, hot then cold, but still had to concentrate on the maths. We were going to be short but if we changed money on the black market, and used our personal spending money, we might just scrape through. We gathered from the hotel owner that the 'black' money was 'laundered' by airline crews who took it to Hong Kong and Singapore, or by the 'back door' by corrupt bank officials. So we set up a deal.

The next day the money changer came to the hotel on a scooter looking serious. He declined to remove his crash helmet, and refused to do the deal there in the hotel. He insisted that we go to his house. Harry and Steve Findlay came with me as bodyguards and we weaved our way into the heart of the old quarter along ever more sordid alleyways. Finally, we were beckoned furtively into a black passageway, half expecting to be set upon, and entered a dark and dirty house. The two thousand six hundred pounds was split between us and it was extracted with difficulty from half a dozen bodily hiding places, and the deal done. We counted every rupee before leaving.

The bureaucratic process was not helped by the fact that the Chinese Premier came on a state visit and everything closed for a day, but eventually we met our three Sherpas, who frankly were not impressed by the new and second hand gear we had brought for them. There were also some tough negotiations on pay before it all ended in smiles, handshakes and promises to get us to the summit. Ours was to be a 'Joint Expedition' because no Nepalese had ever climbed Cho Oyu either, which meant that we paid the peak fee, trekking permit fee, import licence, customs duties, Sherpa insurance, provided pay, food and lodging for the Sherpas and Liason Officer, gave them all the gear they needed, tents and sleeping bags, and they gave us in return nothing but bureaucratic hassle.

As well as the paperwork there was all the fresh food for the walk-in to buy in the markets, the loads to pack, two lorries had to be hired, and we had to have the obligatory meeting with Liz Hawley. Liz originally came to Nepal in 1959 and met every expedition as it arrived, and interviewed them when they left. She told us a bizarre story of a Czech expedition who were also planning to climb Cho Oyu on another route at the same time as us. They were being bankrolled by an American woman ex-ambassador to Nepal, who had already paid $15,000 to have their equipment shipped to Kathmandu, but now the climbers had apparently failed to turn up. An American filmmaker was there to join the team but it all looked like it was going to fold.

Finally, we climbed onto the back of our lorry, the other having gone ahead already, for the twelve and a half hour journey to Jiri, where we crashed in some rough hotel, all suffering the shits and Ned with a mild fever.

CHAPTER 10

The honest Bank Manager and other Dilemmas

AT THE START THERE WERE 86 LOADS, though at the end of the first day we realized that some porters were carrying very light loads, and after re-packing and weighing we managed to pay off some of the 'extras'. Every rupee counted. Our head Sherpa, Long, also suggested that we employ a Sherpa specifically to be at the very back to make sure no porters ran off with any loads. We had heard on the climbing grapevine that this was a common enough practice so we agreed. Always there seemed to be little extra costs creeping into the frame.

The next ten days of the expedition to Namche Bazar though were the most enjoyable. Sunny days, laughing and joking with our Sherpas and porters, up and down across the grain of the country, crossing a succession of passes, camping out in pretty countryside, learning something of the Sherpa way of life. A characteristic of Sherpas is their mischievousness. One lunch hour a group of porters lay sleeping on the grass and our lads tied all the shoe laces together; when they were shouted at to get up they all fell over, much to the amusement of the perpetrators.

The Liaison Officer was a pain in the backside though. Another bureaucrat only with us to get the most out of us that he could. He complained at regular intervals about the quality of his kit, that he didn't have a radio to listen to, and that some of his clothing was not brand new. We noticed that he toadied up to the two junior Sherpas, Dorje and Pemba, no doubt sowing ill seeds with them. We got to a point where we just ignored him. The other nagging problem was that most of us were still suffering from the inconvenient effects of the Kathmandu quickstep. Away from the contaminated water and filthy hygiene of the hotel, and now enjoying Sherpa cooking, thankfully this didn't last too long.

Typically at the crack of dawn we would listen to Long Tenzing circling the camp chanting his Buddhist prayers, dispelling the evil demons, and then we would catch the pungent smell of him burning juniper for the Gods. Next Kami the cook boy would come round with 'bed tea' and washing water. He had the widest grin on the most innocent face it has ever been my pleasure to tease unmercifully. In the evening we always asked him "Apple pie Kami?" to which he usually replied, "No Appie pie Sahib". We would groan and laugh and he would nearly do himself serious damage just by smiling.

As we approached Namche word came through that a Sherpa had been killed on the Indian Women's Everest expedition. Our Sherpas knew the man. It was there and then that I started to understand that death on the mountains, especially in the Everest region, is a yearly fact of life. There are not so many Sherpa villages and everyone seems to know everyone else. To the Sherpa community big expeditions such as ours meant good wages, money to be made from used oxygen cylinders and second-hand expedition gear, maybe travel abroad, as well as status, and even foreign girlfriends if they got lucky, but the risks were enormous. What would it be like to work in an industry where you played Russian roulette every day? How long could the Sherpa ethos of bravery and service with a smile last against such attrition I wondered. Leaving England we had just assumed that all Sherpas would be loyal, wedded to the cause, team players of distinction, but would the ones picked for us by our Nepalese ground handler be as good as we hoped for? We were counting on their strength. The days on trek slid by and the friendship grew.

A day out from Namche our head Sherpa, Long Tenzing, had alerted me to the fact that when we came to pay off the porters we would need small denomination notes, and therefore he and I would have to rush ahead of the rest to catch the one bank in Namche before closing time. On the last day Long and I started early and at the entrance to the National Park, at the foot of the will-sapping climb up to the Sherpa capital, I noticed there was a sign listing all the rules. Rule No. 1 was 'no littering' and right next to the sign there was a slope leading down to the river covered in rubbish thrown out of the office by the Park Wardens. Caring for the environment had barely reached the awareness of trekkers or the Nepalese at this time. The Kleenex Trail was well named. We carried on up the steep path in strong sunshine and unexpectedly rounding a corner there was my first view of Everest. Whoever you are, the first view of the tallest mountain on our planet is a memorable event. I remember it as being ever so slightly disappointing; there was no way of judging the scale, as only the very top poked out over the Lhotse/Nuptse ridge. I had wanted to be dumfounded by its size.

As Namche came into sight we rounded one final corner and there was a wizened old woman spinning her prayer wheel. It was Long's mother who had come out to meet him. At that time there were no telephones in the Solu Khumbu region but the news of his arrival and our expedition had spread almost as quickly by word of mouth.

Namche is a place of eagles, crows and Lammergeiers, set in an amphitheatre of soaring snow peaks. The streets are rough stone, the municipal dustman does his rounds rarely, Sherpa houses are occupied by livestock, humans and the occasional flea. Incense burns, monks pass you in the street, shopkeepers look longingly at you, mangy dogs avoid you in case you kick them, and everyone puts their hands together and greets you with 'Namaste'.

Long took me to his house where I met his wife, who he shared with his brother. I was greeted with a silk scarf and given Tibetan tea, tipped carefully from a three foot high wooden and brass urn, where it had been slooshing and swashing. I felt so happy and at ease sitting in their smoke-blackened living room with its copper pots and pans, dishevelled children and ear to ear smiles. Long was older than the other two climbing Sherpas, and we had come to understand that his wife did not want him to go above Base Camp. He had hinted to us though that he would go further. We could see Long would be the organizing power; he was a cut above the other two. There was something almost aristocratic about Long. True, he and his close friend the cook had an eye to making money, and they made sure that their relations got jobs

Sherpa Long Tenzing's mother as we arrived at Namche Bazar.

as porters before everyone else, and that we sold them our cast-off equipment at the end of the expedition, but still that was all business. He was always fair and honest. Dorje was the playboy, good looking, strong, but lazy and not very bright. Pemba was middle aged and difficult to fathom. He had that habit of not looking me in the eye when I talked to him; something that does not auger well for an instinctive friendship.

After salt-butter tea Long and I hurried over to the small bank where a small, neat man, every inch a bank manager, treated the scruffy Westerner with far more respect than he deserved. I handed him a large box containing forty five thousand rupees and asked for small denominations in return. He hurried off saying that it might take some time. After half an hour he appeared with several much larger boxes stuffed with old twenty rupee notes. Time was running on and there was no way I could count that much small change. I took his word for it that it was correct. Long was my witness in any case. No sooner had we got back to Long's house than the seventy four porters started to arrive, dumping their loads all over the place, laughing and smiling. It was wonderful chaos and a happy, sad affair paying them their money. Pay day is a serious affair, with speeches, gaiety, endless cups of Chang (barley beer) and every rupee counted and thumb print receipts given. Respect is shown from both sides, and by God these men are strong. I had tried one of their loads using the traditional head strap method and lasted barely ten minutes. A couple of the strongest young men carried double loads for double pay. In 1984 we were young bucks, only the middle-aged and the elderly worry about slipped disks; it just did not occur to us then that double loading was a crime against humanity.

In Long's house smoke billowed, drunken men laughed, women made a vain attempt at keeping order, to be repaid with ribald comments which they clearly enjoyed. All of us carefully avoided the horns of the clearly pissed off yak which stood just outside Long's front door. Long had generously asked us to stay in his house. All the gear was stacked on the ground floor, with the animals, while we enjoyed true Sherpa hospitality and a bottle of our sponsor's Glorious Twelfth whisky on the first floor. Rough, tough life is so much more real, so much more pleasurable than the polite correctness of the West. We revelled in it.

Next morning I looked again at the money and discovered I was thirteen thousand rupees short of what I imagined we needed to take with us to pay the yak men. So off we went to the bank again to change some more dollars, only to be met by a very embarrassed and worried bank manager. He had discovered that they had short changed us.

There was a strange scene where he tried to discover how much we thought we were missing, and I was on the one hand deeply suspicious of some grand fiddle, and on the other amazed and grateful that they were owning up to something they could easily have kept quiet about. They handed me back ten thousand rupees. Rarely has my faith in human nature been so completely reinforced.

In town there were formalities to be endured. We checked in at the local Police station where I was interested to see that Mickey Mouse had beaten me yet again. We filled in the forms here and at the National Park HQ, where we were told they had a solar powered radio. It only worked if the sun was shining. If it wasn't working we were told you had to bribe the police to use theirs.

The day was marred by a fantastic row with the Liason Officer who had seen us in the market buying cigarettes for the Sherpas. He came over to me and said that if we didn't buy him some he would start to enforce the Rules and Regulations for various things. I told him not to try blackmailing me and that this was supposed to be a joint expedition. I said so far we had been expected to pay for everything, and launched into a huge and growing list, including his own food, accommodation and his pay. I told him, politely, that I thought it was a cheek to expect us to pay for his personal cigarettes as well. He started to argue back and I pointed out that it was his first expedition, and that we were being more than generous, and basically I told him I would listen to no more. The flare up had been exacerbated by the fact that the previous day he had tried to get me to buy the Nepalese flag that had to be flown at Base Camp. I had thought that as a Joint Expedition the least they could do would be to buy their own flag. It was clear by now he was not intending to climb with us on the expedition, and I now waited for him to find an excuse to stay behind in the comfort of an hotel or a lodge. To his credit he stayed on at Base Camp for at least half the expedition. In fairness to the poor chap we knew he could not climb with us, he just did not have the skills or the fitness. He wanted to though and we had to refuse to take the responsibility for him. It was rather sad actually that halfway through the trip he suddenly asked for a rope, ice axe, crampons and a helmet. I asked him why he wanted these things as he knew he couldn't climb with us. He replied that he needed them for 'prestige' to put outside his tent. In reality he wanted them to sell at the end.

The next day the yaks turned up, were gingerly loaded and we were off again. The expedition herd blundered through the bazaar, up the hill and along the Everest Base Camp trail. Shortly we turned left to cross the Mon La Pass and later in the day camped in a clearing above a noisy river. Next morning the yak handlers were up early attempting to assemble the thirty three reluctant yaks which clearly wanted to be anywhere else except tied up in our camp. Suddenly a large group of them charged through the campsite. Unfortunately a large male went right through one of the sleeping tents, flattening it. The person inside emerged swearing and cursing, but unharmed. 'Ned' Kelly, one of England's finest examples of how to behave as a gentleman, and who in the most stressful situations appeared never to be the slightest bit ruffled, really lost his temper. It was not the time to laugh at his expense, though we did all fall about afterwards. Ned had been loaned to us by BBC Bristol to film up to as far as Base Camp. He was a producer/ cameraman for the Natural History Unit, but had also climbed twice with Bonington's Everest South West Face expeditions, reaching 26,000ft/7,900 metres in 1975. Our regional BBC wanted to make a half hour feature about our climb. Ned would film as far as Base Camp, and the rest of us would take turns in filming above the snow line. Unfortunately for us Ned had other commitments which prevented him joining the climb itself.

That same morning we had woken to urgent cries of "Cho Oyu's in sight, come and look," and there she was, the Turquoise Goddess as the Sherpas call her, far higher above our neck bent heads than seemed reasonable. Our time of pleasant walking through Nepal's sculpted hillsides was about to end and serious danger was a mere few days away. It was simultaneously exciting and sobering. Knowing, significant looks were exchanged. However, the next two days were about as idyllic as it can be. We took our sweating bodies, here today gone tomorrow, past mountains built to impress, whose awesome magnitude made us feel humble. We ate cheesecake, slid around on a frozen lake, and slowly but surely more and more of Cho Oyu unfolded before our dazzled eyes. We were not too shy to look, and all was well until the day before Base Camp when human greed spoilt the plot.

In a deliberate, blatant rip-off the yak men and porters demanded two days' wages to take us on to the crossing point of the Ngzumpo Glacier, and yet we had received, the night before, a handwritten message from Matt telling us that it was two and a half hours from where we were. It was a game of bluff; we were trying to hang onto our money, they were trying every trick they knew to take it from us. Not far from where we were camped was a whole herd of yaks and quietly we approached the owner who was, at first, keen to take us. Our guys must have got wind that we were aiming to send them packing because the new yak owner suddenly went off the idea. It did have the effect of knocking the price down though. This round they won and we moved slowly on to Base Camp, a mile or two from the truly stupendous South Face, down which avalanches poured at fairly regular intervals.

CHAPTER 11

So Near and yet so Far

AFTER THE RIP-OFF by the yak men we reached the slag heap that was Base Camp, to the major shock that there just wasn't an objectively safe route to climb Cho Oyu on this side of the mountain. No-one would be stupid enough to try the stupendous South Face leading directly to the summit, and so our plan was to gain Cho Oyu's long East Ridge from a gigantic plateau away east of the South Ridge.

Between us and the huge snow plateau, five thousand feet higher up, there were, at first sight, nothing but icefalls and vertical rock. Above the plateau we could see ridges we could follow; but how were we going to reach the plateau? The reconnaissance trek by Roland Perriment the previous year had been unable to see the bottom half of the climb. Roland had spied the route from a rocky hill called Gokyo Ri some six miles from Cho Oyu and what he had been able to see looked reasonable. The trouble was that views of the bottom half of the climb had been blocked by other mountain ridges. Luckily for Roland he had not been able to join the expedition. We put in considerable effort into trying to find a safe way but there wasn't one. Our eventual route took us across the Ngzumpo Glacier, up a gully of a thousand one hundred feet at the top of which was perched a serac the size of a ten storey block of flats. We next turned left to Camp 1 at 19,300ft/5,883 metres, across a square sloping snowfield we named the 'football pitch', and up through an icefall to the snow plateau. The gully we jokingly called Death Gully. The camp to the left of it was reasonably safe, protected by a rock buttress, though during our time on the mountain three avalanches crossed the football pitch. One was quite sizeable and we watched it go by while we were having breakfast one morning. The route through the icefall was complicated and tenuous. At one point there was an ice tunnel you had to crawl through, there were flimsy snow bridges, steep traverses and long gullies where we fixed ropes to speed our passage.

A certain kind of madness entered the climbing team at this point.

71

Logically we should have turned round and gone off and spent the time usefully in an Ashram on the banks of the Ganges. Strangely the thought did not occur to us. We persuaded each other that really it wasn't so unsafe and that probably nothing had fallen down 'Death Gully' for thousands of years. Sure, it was going to again one day but the odds were pretty good. We would just have to make sure we got up the gully as fast as possible. As far as the icefall was concerned, we had seen worse.

In the months leading up to the expedition I used to drive along in my car roaring Cho Oyu's name. Fired up, exultant, laughing with joy, particularly once the money was raised from a company laughingly called Endless Holdings. Quite simply I love the mountains. Whether it is a weekend in North Wales or a trip to the Himalaya I arrive and always experience the same thing – an emotional outpouring, followed by positive happiness. I would even say it is a tangible physical thing spreading to all parts of my body. I think it is something to do with being made to feel humble. 'Nipper' Harrison said the same thing to me at Base Camp. There they stand for millions of years staring into space vaguely aware of the scurrying humans at their feet, and if the humans itch too much then perhaps they might shake to rid themselves of a nuisance. Certainly the Sherpa people regard them as entities who have great powers, and that love and respect are needed in direct dealings with them. A good Sherpa friend of mine, Kami Tshering, said to me once, "Steve la, you know we Sherpas believe that Everest chose very carefully the first person she allowed to stand on her summit. Our friend Ed Hillary has devoted his life to helping the people of Everest. Other people would not have done this – she chose him carefully for us."

So before we started climbing we held a ceremony to honour the goddess. The Sherpas went to a lot of trouble with this; first erecting a shrine and then a tall pole with prayer flag banners streaming off it, with the Nepalese flag on top. We had forgotten to bring a Union Jack so we made a cardboard one, using strips from a red and blue poly bag. We gathered, we chanted, we threw rice and tsampa in the air, and when we were finished we drank whisky. I wasn't sure the goddess would approve of this but the Sherpas were keen, so we went along with it.

Then we debated. We talked and talked, we went up with binoculars to examine all the possibilities, and then we talked some more. It was a lucid, clearly reasoned, progressive debate but it didn't make anything any safer. With grave misgivings, and still struggling against the altitude we started to climb.

A week of enthusiastic labour had flown by and Death Gully had been climbed by my fellow humans for the first time. Camp 1 had been erected and my turn came round to play Russian roulette in the gully.

The sun beat down and it was like being on a treadmill in a Turkish Bath. My left hand was a useless floppy thing on the end of my loosely dangling arm. My right hand reluctantly carried the axe. I had got into the habit now of gently lifting each cramponed foot just high enough to clear the snow, and pushing it forward a small even step each time. My lips were flabby things, an opening sufficient to suck in the non-existent air. My lungs had never worked so hard; the dry air eventually producing a very sore throat. My lips were burnt, along with the tip of my tongue, the skin around my nostrils, the end of my nose, my cheeks, my forehead and by earlobes. I wasn't going anywhere fast and the sun took advantage. I took small pleasure at picking at these things when I knew no one but God was looking. He didn't care anyway. My head was a boiled vegetable inside a bone pressure cooker. My heart, lungs and legs were taking all the power output, and I wanted to extract more power. I wanted so much to go faster, to get out of this place. Whenever I can feel my pulse in my lips I know I am working at full stretch.

Anger at least provided adrenalin. I had stood at the bottom of 'Death Gully' and the two Sherpas, Dorji and Pemba, had simply refused to go up. To them this was just a job. They were not interested in appeasing the great god of mountaineering history. They dropped their loads and went back to Base Camp. They said it was just too dangerous, never mind the fact that Matt and Jeff had already 'proved' the route the day before, and fixed rope on the steep bits.

Fuming and outraged I had stepped round from the rock buttress at the foot of the gully and looked up. There were the seracs, perfectly white, no doubt edging their way to the drop off. One thousand one hundred feet steeply up the snow and ice in the gully; two hours if I went fast. Fear got me off far too quickly, I slowed. The rocks on either side were polished. I side-stepped up the hard packed snow, eyes furtively looking for a rock to hide behind if the ice blocks came down, false hope. I felt like a Pakistani lorry driver who believes it is Allah's will if he dies in a head-on; it does not stop him from driving ever faster.

A couple of days later in the mess tent, I mentioned I thought the rocks were polished in the gully because stuff must have been regularly falling down it for millions of years. I was told forcibly I was wrong; it was glacial action they said. We all knew it wasn't. Anyway, nothing came down, at least not while any of us was in the gully, except for a rock the size of two footballs which bounced over my head. Our Sherpas held out for a day or two but peer pressure eventually forced their hand. We made no big thing of it and before long we were all the best of friends again. We understood, so did they.

Time passed. Loads moved up Death Gully. We even had two Mormons visit Base Camp and offer to carry loads for us. We felt they were just trying to get their foot inside the tent door and we turned them away. Some of us acclimatised and went faster, others didn't. I remember a night at Camp 1 when 'Nipper' was throwing up every ten minutes, and suffering with a blinding headache. The best rock-climber in the South West of England did not take to altitude. Bitter disappointment reduced my friend to tears and he left early for the fleshpots. Dr. Norman Waterhouse, our ambitious surgeon, who had been desperate to join the Bristol 'gang', and came along at the last moment, suffered the same fate. Steve Findlay, built like a Greek God, gentle and green fingered, made it up onto the plateau at 21,000ft/6,400 metres but he could do no more. Then there was my best friend Harry McAulay who was fine until 19,000ft/5,800 metres but that was always a ceiling he could not break through. In typical fashion he unselfishly decided to stay on and support those still left on the mountain. Not that there were many of us at the end. Illness, whether because of the altitude or because of bad hygiene, reduced the aspirants for the summit to Matt Priestman, Jeff Jackson, Steve Monks, Lydia Bradey and myself. The Sherpas stuck it out except for Pemba who disappeared off to the Kunde medical post. He had thought he had kidney stones but it turned out to be constipation. Long Tenzing was tempted to go higher than Base Camp and even proudly carried up 'Death Gully' to Camp 1, and on up to Camp 2. Dorje, fuelled by a desire for fame, betterment of his climbing CV, and promises of bonuses, looked like having serious summit ambition until he too succumbed to illness and went down from Camp 3.

My most enduring memory of the expedition was the worst night of my life, spent at Camp 2 on 6th May. This was during a period of nine days where I was on my own at Camp 2 and later Camp 3 and trying to carry loads to Camp 4. Violent storms had marooned me. Jeff and Matt were always one camp ahead of me, and Lydia and Monksie always one camp behind. That particular night, after corned beef and mash, I involuntarily did something I had not done since I was ten years old. I hurriedly undressed in the tent, in temperatures around -20°C. It was blowing and snowing and dark outside. No sooner had I re-dressed than the pains became violent and I ended up pissing out my arse onto torn up plastic bags. I could do little else I thought. Back into clothes, struggled into the sleeping bag only for the pains to start all over again. This time I used the saucepan. So it went on, and I was in and out of the sleeping bag and my clothes a further four times. I took some Codeine and felt like death. I wondered whether this would mark the end of my climb. I even contemplated firing a flare. Miraculously at 5.00 a.m. I felt fine again and not willing to contemplate a whole day doing nothing, and knowing that within hours the temperature would be intolerable, I found I was able to carry a load to Camp 3.

Earlier in the expedition, by the flip of a pan lid, I had lost to Jeff the privilege of trying to keep up with Matt. I could see them sometimes; little dots moving ever so slowly upwards. They climbed a sensational series of very steep ice pitches that led from the gigantic plateau, up a subsidiary ridge of Cho Oyu. Then I lost sight of them as they traversed to establish Camp 4, at 23,000ft/7,000 metres, right at the foot of the frankly awesome face that led to a col between Cho Oyu to the west, and Ngozumpa Kang 1, 25,971ft/7,916 metres, to the east. I did my best to follow along behind them taking loads up of stuff I thought they would need. It meant that I had to jumar up their fixed ropes to get to Camp 4. It is a horribly frightening experience trusting your whole weight, and therefore your life, to an anchor put in by someone else and then clamping up that rope for one hundred and sixty feet, before transferring to the next rope and doing it again, with the drop below your feet growing and growing. Sometimes the rope would be a bit icy and the clamp would slip back, giving me a fearful shock each time. One or two of the ice pitches were vertical or near vertical, and the rest were damn steep.

Nine days is a long time to spend on your own, especially when it is all above 21,000ft/6,400 metres, and the weather is bad. To go to the next camp or not to go, that was the question. Would the weather improve or get worse, would the snow be too deep, would I get lost or caught out in a storm? If I stayed in camp would the weather turn to sunshine, and if so I would have wasted a day. In the heat of the day every little thing is a massive effort, and you get screamingly bored. You know every object in the tent, that the left-hand cooker goes better than the right, you read and read, sleep and think. I recall thinking that the whole stupid escapade was dangerous, over-ambitious, not a bloody good laugh, but a load of hassle, that it was a crime against my poor parents and my sister, against my friends, and that I was endangering others merely by persuading them to come with me. Was it my father's severe discipline that made me a rebel or was I just a terrible child? His expectations for me and my brother were too high. Even climbing Nun was not enough, he had to pick fault. Cho Oyu would be the big success. Women, I thought about women. I could be married and settled down. I just laughed to myself at this; it was an alien concept. Was I a failure with women? I didn't think so; I just had not met the right person. Through illness, storms, people leaving to go back to Kathmandu, through doubts as to my reasons for being there, through the danger of snapped bones, torn flesh and death, the fire still burned to stand on the top. In the cold light of day it seemed crazy to risk slowly freezing to death in the bottom of a crevasse with half your bones broken, or to be buried alive under a million tons of snow, or to be blown off a ridge and fall thousands of feet, merely for the pleasure of standing on top of a mountain for a few minutes. Why then do we take such terrible risks? Firstly there is the 'It won't happen to me' syndrome; young men in the prime of life believe they are invincible. They also believe that in extremis they will unfailingly be the perfect decision maker. Neither assumption is anywhere near the mark. Then there is the 'we are doing it for a higher cause'. This is the one that appeals to me most; that mankind has always been adventurous and it is admirable for him to boldly go where no person has gone before. I like this line of reasoning. It is the exploring for the sake of it, and for no other reason, that is the primal urge. Shipton and Tilman were in this category and forsook all comforts both in life, and on the expeditions, to get to that hard, pure ethic. What sacrifices you have to make though to be that 'true explorer'.

Of course, intellectually I knew risking my life to stand on top of a rock was contributing nothing to anything. I really was not doing this for fame either; there is no merit in fame, and money was certainly not the motive. What then? Was my longing to stand on the top like a teenage infatuation for a sexy girl who was just beyond reach? No, it was to do with freedom; to stand outside the tent and watch a storm ten miles away with its centre pulsing, to hear the howling of the wind, to be beyond the reach of anyone as the big bad wolf tried to blow down the house of nylon. I liked the taste of being a free man; to stand outside the rules and regulations, the career, the soft life, the yes sir, no sir of making a living to pay the mortgage.

The summit looked so close now, just a few thousand feet. It was still attainable; there was no thought of giving up. There was also another subliminal force that fuelled the inner rage, made me angry, made me determined. It was the sad, sad fact that my brother Richard, who had stood on the top of Nun with me, had died tragically two years previously. On the eve of the anniversary of his death, alone in my tent, emotion I had kept in check overcame me and I wept for him. I was doing this for him. On my last load carry I had scared myself badly. Setting off at 5.30 a.m. I had reached to within seventy yards of Camp 4 by early afternoon. I had a thumping headache and as on Nun Kun I had got to that point of exhaustion where my legs felt like jelly. Dark clouds were moving in, and the traverse from the top of the fixed ropes at twenty three and a half thousand feet had all been gradually downhill for a long way. I started to doubt that I would have the energy to get back to the top of the ropes, the weather would move in, the snow would fill my tracks and that would be it. I wanted to get to Matt and Jeff's camp, but my life seemed more important. I dumped the load and turned round. I had, however, seen the two black dots moving towards the final wall and knew they must be making their summit bid. Completely shattered I made it back to Camp 3 just as it started snowing. Monksie, Lydia and Dorje had finally caught up with me, and there they were at Camp 3. I was so pleased to see friends again, and in between severe coughing fits, I told them of the route ahead. Dorje though was ill and waved goodbye to us and his summit chances on the 15th. It was particularly galling from him as word had come through that his brother-in-law had just summitted Everest.

Camp 4 on Cho Oyu. Everest in the distance.

It was now or never. We three set off after Matt and Jeff from Camp 3 on 16th. There were two tents up there now and enough food but we were in a sorry state. I had spent a month now above 6,400 metres and had lost almost two stone off my meagre ten and a half stones. I was skeletal, and inwardly now knew I did not have the physical strength left for a shot myself. Monksie was ill and getting worse. I think the fact that he and Lydia had cooked in their tent with the door mostly closed that first night at Camp 4 was largely to blame. It burnt the oxygen and gave off fumes – not a good idea at that altitude. You have to leave the door open. The next morning Steve was groggy, listless and with a bad head whereas he had been on good form when we arrived. A rest day is

The rotten rock gullies that Matt and Jeff could not get past.   *Photo: Matt Priestman*

TOP East Kulu Expedition 1977. Front row L to R: Roland Perriment, Barry Needle, Steve Berry. Back Row: Tara Chand, Dawn Bean, George Crawford-Smith. *Photo: Paul Bean* BOTTOM Advance Base Camp. Mt Devachan behind, Mt Papsura with Roland and Barry's impressive South West Ridge. OVERLEAF Views from the summit of Angdu Ri.

TOP Houseboats, Srinagar, Kashmir.   BOTTOM The royal palace of Leh.

TOP Nun expedition members. Bottom row L to R: Barry Needle, Neelam Kumar (Liaison Officer), Steve Berry. Back row: Ghulam Rasool, Richard Berry, Norman Croucher, Steve Monks, Damian Carroll, John Margesson. *Photo: Steve Berry Collection* BOTTOM A tricky river crossing.

TOP Ladakhi porters in bare feet. Neelam Kumar, our Liaison Officer, third from right.   BOTTOM Near Camp I on Nun. Mt Zanskar I behind.

TOP Nearing the summit of Nun, 23,410ft/7,135 metres.   BOTTOM John Margesson on the summit of Nun. *Photo: Barry Needle*

TOP LEFT Ringdom gompa in 2008.   TOP RIGHT The 'precious ruler' of Padum, Phuntshok Dawa, and his wife Dolma at their house in 1987 in the kingdom of Zanskar.   MIDDLE The Cho Oyu Expedition Sherpa team 1984. Kneeling: Long Tenzing. Back row: Cook boy, Nawang our cook, Dorji, Pemba and Kami.   BOTTOM Cho Oyu from Base Camp.   OPPOSITE Climbing through the ice fall on Cho Oyu. OVERLEAF Nearing Camp II on Cho Oyu.

OPPOSITE Jeff Jackson hitting the East Ridge, Cho Oyu. *Photo: Matt Priestman*   TOP LEFT Steep ice between Camp III and Camp IV, Cho Oyu.   TOP RIGHT Jeff Jackson and Matt Priestman at Camp IV after the summit bid.   BOTTOM At the bottom of Death Gully.   OVERLEAF Mt Gangkar Punsum, Bhutan.

TOP Kathmandu. BOTTOM The Tashichhodzong, Thimphu, Bhutan. OPPOSITE Paro Dzong, Bhutan.

OPPOSITE Loading the horses at the beginning of the trek to Gangkar Punsum. *Photo: Ginette Harrison*
TOP Yaks on trek.   MIDDLE LEFT Leaping dancer at the Thimphu tsechu.   MIDDLE RIGHT The hot springs at Dur Sachu.   BOTTOM The Bhutan Expedition 1986. Bottom row L to R: Lydia Bradey, Jeff Jackson, Steve Berry. Standing: Ginette Harrison, Steve Findlay, Harry McAulay, Steve Monks. *Photo: Steve Berry Collection*   OVERLEAF Heading back along the 'dinosaur' ridge towards Camp I.

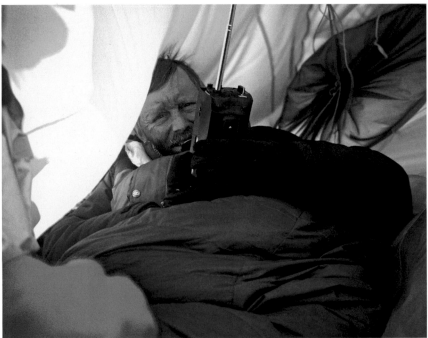

TOP Camp I on Gangkar Punsum before the storm. BOTTOM Trying to contact Base Camp on the radio from the wrecked tent at Camp I. *Photo: Alan Jewhurst*

TOP Ginette Harrison.   BOTTOM Helicopter arrives at Base Camp.

ABOVE Dancer at the king of Bhutan's birthday celebrations at the end of the Bhutan expedition.

not a rest day at 23,000ft/7,000 metres; it's a torture. It is so so hot and yet the water in your water bottle stays frozen. We roasted from 6.00 a.m. until the afternoon clouds moved in, and we could no longer keep watch for Matt and Jeff. There had been no sign of them all day, and the walkie-talkies we had brought were useless up here. It must mean they were on the summit ridge. I had managed to walk the seventy yards to pick up the load I had dumped and that had just about done me in. It took me an hour to get there and back. The views were the only enjoyable thing up there. At Camp 4 we looked down into a basin bigger and deeper than anything I had seen before. Gyachung Kang a touch under 26,000ft/8,000 metres, stood opposite scraping the jetstream with its cliffs of impossibility. Fifteen miles away, and looking small was the North Face of Everest. Monksie had now deteriorated to the point of vomiting. We knew we had to go down.

At 4.00 p.m. Matt stumbled through the mist. They had climbed the wall, bivouacking in a bergschrund twice on the way, and then higher up in a snow hole, until they emerged onto the East Ridge into the teeth of a gale. It had involved some very hard ice climbing at 25,000ft/7,600 metres and they had arrived late in the day, luckily finding a crevasse they could crawl into for the night. They got up at 11.00 p.m. and emerged only to find ferocious, unrelenting, numbing wind. At first light, 4.00 a.m., they tried again convinced now that the summit was only three hours away, and a mere formality. Hard frozen snow meant they made fast progress; thirty or forty steps at a time. Then, unbelievably, they rounded a corner to be faced with a colossal system of gullies, with steep sloping rocks dropping thousands of feet into Tibet. They had tried to cross two hundred feet below the ridge, nearly falling off in the process. Great disappointment came like a shadow. We had failed. Monksie had to be helped down, my legs were so thin now they would hardly support me and a heavy rucksack going downhill, Matt had frostbite in some fingers and didn't recover until he got back to England and decent medical care. There was no one to partner Lydia who still wanted to go on.

The next day we got down to Camp 3. Steve was still vomiting. The day after we stopped at Camp 2. He was still vomiting. After that he was his old self again. Thank God for the best weather on the trip. The once in a lifetime views started to disappear and the cracked surface of the bottom glacier slowly came up to meet us. The icefall had changed beyond recognition. At one point we had to jump a deep crevasse, having thrown the sacks across first, where previously there had been a bridge of ice. Halfway down the icefall Monksie and I were in a constricted gully and there was a very loud crash of collapsing ice above us, very loud. Luckily the avalanche chose not to come down our gully. At Camp 1 the tent was fifty yards away in a heap with all the contents strewn around the place. Was this sheer carelessness by the Sherpas or had some animal been here? We would never find out.

I was the problem by now. I had to rest more and more, even when abseiling. Matt and Jeff had long since disappeared over the horizon. We got to Death Gully to find that something big had fallen down cutting all the fixed ropes and leaving behind a lot of rocks and small ice blocks. Fear is a great motivator and we shot down the gully. The last obstacle was the glacier at the bottom which we had to cross to get to Base Camp. Normally this was nothing; a stroll in the park. Steve and Lydia slowly drew ahead and disappeared too. The white of the glacier meant that it was a frying pan. I staggered forward trying to follow their vague trail. I was chaff in a gale. I kept going a few steps at a time in a daze, and got lost. It seemed like hours later I got to the far side of the glacier but some ice cliffs barred my way. There was no way I had the energy to turn round and go back so I started to climb down. A handhold broke off and I fell backwards. By sheer luck I only went ten feet and made a perfect landing, not twisting or breaking anything. Had I injured myself with darkness approaching I would have been in serious trouble. The shock of this fact hit me as soon as I had picked myself up, but I managed to quell the shaking before it started. It was the final problem though and I knew I could find my way now. Down at Base the others had realized something was wrong and Jeff had come out to find me. He took my sack, and after some blurred conversation he left me behind. When I finally did pull into camp I broke down into floods of tears and just could not stop. Relieved to be alive, to be safe again at last, distressed that it was over and we had failed. I was presented with a plate of roast potatoes, beans and rice. Next day, after I had recovered, a huge wave of relief and joy filled me. The world was open to me again, death was behind. I lay in the tent thinking how pleased my parents would be, listened to The Police and Pink Floyd, and laid plans for the future.

To be honest The Bristol Cho Oyu expedition was not a landmark in mountaineering history. We failed by a few hours to reach the summit and were defeated by a series of near vertical rotten rock gullies at twenty six thousand feet, which we just couldn't get past. We were just another failed expedition. We lived for a few brief weeks at the extreme end of intensity, and thankfully no one got killed. They could have easily been. Every day we spent climbing we were spinning the chamber and pulling the trigger, not even knowing how many bullets there were in the gun. We didn't think of it as a failure though. We had got to within a smidgen of the summit on the world's sixth highest mountain on a new route. We would have made it but for the gullies. I confess it gave us all a bit of pleasure in the years to come to see other teams have a go and also fail.

CHAPTER 12

Getting into Bhutan

BACK IN KATHMANDU after Cho Oyu we brushed our teeth, washed the clothes that we had not taken off for the forty six days we had spent above Base Camp, got rid of the fleas, stuffed our faces, and battled again with the bureaucracy. To no great surprise the Liason Officer had filed a complaint against us. He had reported that we had climbed a peak for which we did not have permission, Ngozumpa Ri. This was backed up by a signed statement to that effect by Pemba, the shifty Sherpa, and worse still by Dorje, who we thought was our friend. The other Sherpas, Long, the cook and Kami, I am pleased to say would have no part in it. Ngozumpa Ri is a bump on the ridge that connects Cho Oyu to Gyachung Kang. Had Matt and Jeff turned right instead of left when they got to the top of the awesome wall they could have in theory climbed it. They most certainly did not though. In fact Pemba and the LO at Base Camp would not have been able to see what they were doing, even through binoculars. They simply manufactured the story. It took some time to convince the authorities of our side of the saga, and to begin with they had confiscated our passports. They also demanded twelve thousand rupees for an extra peak permit. We eventually managed to prove our innocence by reading extracts from our diaries. We did not get our passports back until half an hour before the flight check-in time.

We were also accused of not having a film permit, which was true. We had made a full application for one from England, and had chased the Ministry but had had no reply. On arrival in Kathmandu our agent had said not to bother with it, and after ten days' battling with the main permit, and desperate to get out of the capital, we had left it undone. Now the Ministry wanted $500. After some plea bargaining we eventually settled at $200.

I also spent hours in another Ministry trying to get a deposit refunded. We had to prove that some of our more valuable equipment had not been sold, and was going to leave Nepal with us. The problem with bureaucracies like the Ministry of Tourism is that each layer of officialdom is frightened of the layer above it. Paralysis sets in where the officers are frightened of doing or saying the wrong thing, and the file lies on someone's desk waiting to be cleared. The slight irony was that when we did get the refund it was paid in rupees, and because the Film Permit had to be paid in dollars, and as we were not allowed to take rupees out of the country, and because the official rate of exchange was swingeing we ended up changing it back into dollars on the Black Market.

We were subjected to about a week of these machinations by the authorities. Plenty of time to wallow in the frenetic rush of rickshaws and people, poke our noses into dusty temples, join the shouting throngs in the markets, eat sizzling yak steaks, and meet Liz Hawley again. She came to the new, more hygienic hotel we had switched to and recorded the details of the expedition. At the end she said to me, "…and what next Steven?" I knew exactly what I wanted to do but had been told by countless people that it was quite impossible. "What I would really like to do Liz is climb the highest peak in Bhutan." "Ah well then haven't you met Col. Ongdi yet?" she replied, as though if I was serious I ought to have done by now. I had never heard of him let alone met him. "His office is on Durbar Marg. He is Mr. Bhutan in Kathmandu. If anyone can help you, he can," said Liz.

The next day I had all but forgotten about the conversation when I found myself walking down Durbar Marg, and spotted Col. Ongdi's office. As soon as I walked in the door I knew the omens were good; the hand rail to his office on the first floor was a climbing rope secured to the wall by pitons. There were crossed ice axes hanging on the wall. I was not looking my smartest and the young girl receptionist was a bit sniffy to begin with, but eventually I was shown in to meet the Colonel. He pretended not to notice my attire and we talked for a very long time. Something entirely different emanated from Col. Penjor Ongdi. Asiatic yes, but something more, something subtle, as though he knew something I did not, all the time. He knew all about Gangkar Punsum, 24,770ft/7,550 metres, and my heart missed several beats when he told me it was still unclimbed. He offered to take my application personally to the authorities in Thimphu next month. Little did I realise at the time how this one, almost chance, meeting would change my life completely.

We did, in fact, clear our name, settled the bills, collected our passports and told the taxi driver to drive fast to the airport through the torrential early monsoon downpour. We only just made it up one hill as a stream came flowing down the road towards us. We got on the Biman Bangladesh flight with minutes to spare.

I went back to the other half of my character; the one who had to pay the mortgage. Luckily for him his employers had given him time off for climbing Cho Oyu. They were such a good company they had even given five hundred pounds for Mr. Berry to go off to risk his neck. Very sadly when I got home I was to find that the firm was running into financial difficulties and my job as Land Manager was soon to be redundant. While one half of me applied for the permit for Gangkar Punsum, the other half applied for a job as a Land Manager with a company who built flats for elderly people. Both halves succeeded. The permit was not long arriving via the Colonel, and shortly I started working for a firm I secretly abhorred. They were a mean-minded bunch of slick-suited, shallow-minded provincial developers intent on maximising their profits, and cramming as many 'units' onto each of their developments as they could. They constantly seemed to look for ways of making the flats smaller, and their attitudes pervaded every corner of the firm's thinking. It was a job I needed, but I was not proud to work for them, a little ashamed in fact.

Is it life that is full of coincidences, or is it mountains that produce them? In any case small coincidences, nothing in themselves, showed me I was on the 'right path', and when I was getting bogged down by daily life I would be reminded about Bhutan at regular intervals. Once I had received the permit my father told me that when he had tried to climb Nun, Spencer Chapman had given him the ice axe he had used to make the first ascent of Chomolhari, the second highest peak in Bhutan, though at the time Spencer Chapman thought it was the highest. Much later I discovered that amongst my brother's things was Spencer Chapman's book, *Memoirs of a Mountaineer*, borrowed by my brother from the College of Estate Management library where he had been studying. Spencer Chapman had been a lecturer there and in his hand writing on the inside cover it shows that he had given the book to the library. His accomplished life tragically ended in suicide, as did my brother's. Later still I went on a skiing holiday in France, and after driving from England right across France I entered my hotel room, turned on the television to find a programme on Bhutan just starting. This was in the days when, to my knowledge, there had been nothing about Bhutan on our television at all. Another time on a weekend where I was pursuing a relationship with an attractive girl who lived in Putney, I walked into a travel bookshop to look around, and lo and behold, inside was an exhibition of photos and art from Bhutan. I could have walked into any bookshop in London, but happened by coincidence to stumble in on the only exhibition probably in the country, on the weekend it had started. I am not saying powers beyond my ken were organising these coincidences; perhaps if I had formed an ambition to be the world's greatest snake charmer I would have noticed things connecting me to snakes. In any case fate continued to drip feed me alluring coincidences, and I kept up the momentum to raise the huge sum of money needed.

It was not easy, and having raised most of the cash the permit was cancelled. An American team of international stars and sponsored by Rolex, had obtained a permit ahead of us, but had failed to find Gangkar Punsum and demanded their money back. Their side of the story was that the Bhutanese guides had taken them up the wrong valley. Truth be known the Bhutanese probably did not know which was the 'right' valley. Next there was a strong Japanese team who did find a Base Camp and climbed to about 22,500ft/6,850 metres before one of their climbers suffered high altitude pulmonary odema, and they spent all their energy getting him down. He was helicoptered out and it was some years before they paid the helicopter bill. Lastly, just before us there was an Austrian team who had gone in the monsoon and endured terrible weather and armies of leeches. They also wanted their money back saying they had been badly advised about the time of the year to climb in Bhutan. It was their own fault and pure ignorance on their part. These problems, and the fact that the locals thought the goddess of the mountain was being angered and their yaks were dying of strange illnesses as a result, meant that the villagers had sent a deputation to the king. One minute we had a permit and the next we did not.

We were saved by Doug Scott who knew the British High Commissioner in India and Doug persuaded him to intervene on our behalf. What went on behind the scenes I will never know but miraculously the permit was re-issued. Doug had in fact approached me asking if he could join our team. At the start we were immensely flattered that the John Lennon of the British climbing scene wanted to join us. The problem was Doug wanted to run the expedition in his own way. He wanted to bring on board a famous French climber with the idea that the two of them would climb the mountain entirely 'Alpine style', with the rest of us supporting, or climbing the mountain using two or three camps. Doug is an enigma, a maverick, an idealist, a brave-hearted survivor who was a brilliant climber, and who in an age past, escaped one day from a hippy commune. He was full of some good ideas and, I thought, a lot of dubious ones. Try as we might we did not always see eye to eye, and eventually Doug withdrew from the expedition. Nevertheless, it was a reasonably amicable parting of the ways and since that heady time he has done me a number of good turns and vice versa. In many ways Doug had the last laugh as we failed to make the summit, and a year later he climbed a different and even more beautiful mountain in Bhutan, Jitchu Drake, shortly after Reinhold Messner had failed on it. Jitchu Drake is one of the most beautiful mountains I have ever seen with ridges like razor blades.

One of Doug's more workable ideas for raising money was to invite 'Support Trekkers' along who would pay the expedition a premium for the unique experience of coming into a hitherto practically unexplored region. They would trek as far as Base Camp and then depart. Doug introduced me to a Canadian woman, Maggie Payne, who offered to organise the Support Trek group. All she was looking for, she said, was a free trip and to come along too. She oozed wealth and sex appeal. Her husband was an advisor of some sort to a Sheik in the Middle East and played polo. Maggie? Well we were not quite sure what she did. She was a qualified nurse and accompanied little old rich ladies on long flights around the world, and I think there was some talk of a travel agency office in Saudi Arabia. What the hell; if it was going to raise us much needed money then why not. So we agreed to the scheme little realizing there was a hidden agenda.

The size of our bandobust grew and grew. Eventually we had seven climbers, a four-man film crew, a mental guru for the film crew, a *Sunday Times* Reporter, seven Support Trekkers, Maggie and our darling Press Officer, Tan MacKay. Tan was a single, middle-aged Public Relations manager working for the Reader's Digest. She had bags of humanity and solid determination and got swept up in the romance of what we were doing and where we were going. She raised shed loads of money for us off her own bat. Our expedition Patrons were Chris Bonington and Lord John Hunt. From a rag tag group of Bristol rock-climbers we were now being taken seriously! The money dribbled in. Begging is a difficult profession even when it is dressed up in high ideals and the vagrants put on suits and ties when the need arises. Like all good expeditions we sailed along on a wing and a prayer, and sure enough the last tranche of cash entered the account ten days prior to departure. This cuts a long boring story short, but in any case this time I enjoyed handing in the resignation letter to my exploitative employers, which this time was not devoid of a touch of sarcasm.

CHAPTER 13

Some of the Truth

WHERE LADAKHI PEAK WAS ABOUT NAIVETY AND A CLOSE SHAVE, Nun the best adventure ever and a success, Cho Oyu a horribly dangerous and bitter disappointment, Bhutan was intensely about money, mystery and relationships. The climb itself was also in another league; a harder, fiercer, more daunting challenge, but our team of Bristol climbers had every right to believe we were as capable as anyone else on the British climbing scene. We had all climbed rock and ice virtually every weekend and every holiday since we were in our late teens. Steve Monks had soloed the Eiger North Face, Lydia had by now climbed the world's thirteenth highest peak, Gasherbrum II, and we were this time joined by Dr. Ginette Harrison who went on to become the second British woman to climb Everest and the first woman in the world to climb the third highest peak, Kangchenjunga on the borders of Nepal and Sikkim. Jeff Jackson had reached 26,000ft/8,000 metres on Cho Oyu, and though Steve Findlay was first and foremost a world class rock-climber he was equally brave with two ice axes in his hands. That left Harry McAulay and me. Harry knew from the outset that altitude might be a problem. Harry was talented and super fit, but we all knew 'Aich' might occupy a support role. Me? Well I had a lot of altitude experience by then, but I was never a lead climber. Generally if one of my friends could lead a pitch I could follow it, but not always. I was nowhere in the same class as Monksie, Finders or Capt. Kathmandu (one of our nicknames for Jeff), but I was in with a chance of getting high on the mountain, even the top if my luck panned out.

There was no way we could run this expedition on a shoestring, no way we could shave costs, or haggle our way to the bottom line. The need for a lot of money to pay the high peak fees and Bhutan tourist tax meant a lot of stress and meetings with potential sponsors and filmmakers from one end of the UK to the other. It meant we had to take on board things we did not necessarily welcome as climbers. It's the same problem for all climbers with ambition; it's a treadmill of bigger and harder, more sensational objectives to produce the publicity which will attract the sponsors, which will sell the book and pump the lecture tour, until the next even bigger trip. All we wanted to do was have the adventure. We were worried particularly that a film crew would slow us up, interfere with our game plan, and be asking us every ten minutes to, "Sorry sweetie, be a dear and go back and do that again." Actually it wasn't like that at all. The strains came from within our own group.

However, the mystery of Bhutan was better than twentieth century man could ever imagine. As soon as we landed in Bhutan in a cloud of dust and flying pebbles, with everyone clapping and shouting with relief, and got out the twin prop aircraft, it was just like going back in time.

Capt. Kathmandu and I were the advance party this time and flew with the kit to Calcutta. It was good to be back to the sweet smell, the revolving fans, the Ambassador cars, the heat, the humidity, the sacred cows, the mildewed buildings and the army of grinning taxi drivers at the airport exit, each with his own trick to catch your attention. Had I not been so tired I would even have been amused by the Customs Officer who took us into a separate room in the hope of getting a 'present' for waving off the formalities quickly. Acting confused, pretending not to understand, and lavishing compliments on the said official, I managed to have us waved through anyway. We had been invited to 'stay' at a minor 'palace' near the airport, belonging to Bhutan, which used to be the private residence of their late assassinated Prime Minister. Now it was part occupied by some Bhutanese customs officials and the maintenance crew for Bhutan's two ageing, seventeen-seater Dornier aircraft. Most of the marbled interior was empty and derelict, and the swimming pool was full of weed, and frogs. It was a breeding ground for voracious mosquitoes, which kept me awake at night as they searched for a chink in the mosquito netting. The maintenance crew became great friends and constantly complained of the difficulty of keeping their aircraft airworthy. We played badminton with them every evening on the scraggy lawn. During the sweltering heat of the day we ran hither and thither around Dum Dum airport signing forms and pleading with Customs officials to release our cooking gas. They twirled their hands and nodded their heads, in the wonderful Indian way which says either 'Who knows, the Gods perhaps but not me' or 'We agree this is most unjust but what to do'. Finally we packed all the gear onto a Bhutanese lorry which hopefully would take it overland to Thimphu,

the capital of Bhutan. JJ and I were going to fly in. The flights into
Bhutan in those days regularly got cancelled. We met a group of French
who had been stuck in Calcutta for a week. We were lucky, there was
only one days' delay for us.

The plane flew at 11,000ft/3,350 metres, at 160 knots, out across the
plains of India, until Everest poked out through the clouds, and then we
were droning and vibrating our way up a steep valley, looking down on
houses clinging to hillsides, past a fortress that seemed the size of a
matchbox, in and out of puffy clouds, and past cascading waterfalls.
Steep banking had us clinging to our seats and then there was
Paro Dzong, the castle of 'a pile of Treasures' dominating the valley.
The 'airport' was basically one large ornate shed with dragon flies flitting
about. Peace and tranquillity prevailed. Prayer flags scented the air with
good thoughts. We were in on Col. Ongdi's secret; he knew he was
from a mystical place, and that reality was different in Bhutan.

We were high on adrenalin from the flight, from the build up over
two years, but still the sheer beauty of this private kingdom seemed
unreal. Everyone was dressed in national costume and smiled in the
same way as Col. Ongdi. We were met by a guide, Khangdu Dorji who
had just climbed with a Japanese team on some smaller peaks near
Gangkar Punsum. It was there and then that we discovered that there
had just been an Austrian team attempting 'our' peak. We felt relief at
their failure and amusement at their apparent stupidity at coming in the
monsoon. The fact that they were here at all must have been kept from us,
as Maggie had already been on a recce for a week to meet the authorities
in Thimphu.

We drove to the Olathang Hotel, the first hotel built in Bhutan,
at the time of the fourth king's coronation. JJ and I were given a spacious
chalet each in the grounds. A few cattle with bells mooched under the
pine trees. Inside there were Tibetan carpets, Bhutanese woven fabrics,
and the walls and ceilings were painted with Buddhist symbols, gods,
and dragons in relief. After a lunch in which chillies played a large part,
we were taken for a visit to the Dzong. Built in the early 1600s by the first
ruler, Nawang Namgyal (the Shabdrung), it loomed massive, impregnable
and almost inviolate. I felt so in awe that I was aware that the tone of
my voice was subdued and held respect. A place where time had stood
still and only mighty events such as war, fire or the highest intrigue
could ever change the status quo. Happy, smiling boy monks in groups
chanted prayers by rote, others, bored, lay asleep on window sills.
The floorboards were practically whole tree trunks, gargoyles spat water

off the main roof, Tibetan style decoration and wall paintings were everywhere. We drifted slowly, feeling self conscious, overpowered by its beauty. JJ and I exchanged incredulous expressions across a courtyard. A gong sounded repeatedly, the boys drifted out of an inner temple, and an older monk thrashed a large leather whip against a spot on the floor worn away by centuries of ritual. Eventually we left. It was like coming out of a cinema after the best ever blockbuster.

We headed down the hill and met an old man who posed for photographs and then held out his hand. We feigned ignorance, conscious that here was a sign of Western influence. He and we passed it off as a joke and continued to enjoy each other's company, but I wondered sadly how long it might be before Europeans would be viewed as principally a source of income, and how long it would be before a refusal to pay would be treated with a show of unfriendliness, such as occurs in parts of Nepal and India. We returned to the hotel.

At 7.00 p.m. I called for Jeff and found him deliriously ill, shaking like a leaf, and curled up in a ball. It was difficult to get any sense out of him as he rambled most of the time, but there were lucid moments. He said the fever had hit him like a hammer, with electricity coming out of his hands, feet and head. He said he had spots in front of his eyes and asked me where the people had gone who had erected a plant to give him shelter, and who had put leaves in his mouth. I called the staff, then the manager. The staff showed obvious fear and said it was a well-known bad spirit in the valley. The doctor prescribed some pills and said it was a local fever. I slept on the floor of his room as he seemed in such a bad state and continued to spout delirious babble all night. In the morning he was marginally better and within forty eight hours was recovered.

We didn't get off to an auspicious start in Bhutan. Maggie, Tan and one of our trekkers had arrived ahead of the rest of us and were up in the capital, hoping to complete a few days' trekking to help with their acclimatisation to altitude. When Jeff had recovered we drove up there to join them, only to find that the support trekker, Harry Jensen, was missing. He had become separated from Maggie and Tan in the jungle above Thimphu, when they took a wrong turning and got themselves lost. By the time we found this out it was already dark and he was out there with no warm clothing, no sleeping bag and no food. Already the king had been informed and his permission sought to search his grounds, as our Bhutanese friends thought that if he found a way out of the forest he was bound to end up at the king's palace. The royal bodyguard had even helped in the search. The Ministry of Tourism was highly embarrassed. Maggie and Tan had retraced their route once the jungle turned into steep cliffs. Stupidly Harry had carried on, climbing down steep drops, following a stream, on his own. That night we went to bed at midnight wondering whether he would be alive in the morning. Our new Bhutanese friends were less worried about the freezing temperature and more concerned he would be attacked by a bear. They said that at this time of the year many came down to go scrumping for apples in the orchards in the valley.

Once asleep I had two virtually identical dreams. In the first I was at a party in the hotel with all the expedition and Harry suddenly turned up alive. We were having a whale of a time. In the second I was at the party and everyone was drinking and laughing and there was music, but Harry was still missing. I was called to the back of the hotel where a car was jacked up and someone I did not recognise was under the car trying to change a wheel. The car was on a slope and threatened to topple over and would surely crush the man under the car. A Bhutanese climbed into the car and started the engine. The car was now trying to move forward. The bonnet was up and I had my hand on the throttle control keeping it at idle. As soon as I let go the engine revved up and the car started to move, and I could not get the driver to turn off the engine, even by shouting.

I woke up in a sweat and realised immediately what the dream meant. I needed to be in control, and at the moment I wasn't. Harry had last been seen descending small cliffs, which looked to the ladies like they were getting bigger. Maybe he had fallen, broken a leg, or worse. JJ and I were the only rock-climbers in Bhutan at that moment. I had been a member of Cheddar Cliff Rescue Team years back, Jeff was a paramedic. Obviously it was us who had to go down through the same forest to find Harry. I got Maggie out of bed. She knew the right people to call. At 2.30 a.m. we rang the Director of Bhutan Tourism Corporation, Jigme Tshultim, and I explained my fears. He agreed. At 5.30 a.m. we collected ropes, clothing and food from our stores and set off. Maggie gave clear instructions as to where it had been where they had lost the main trail, and a detailed description of the jungle, stream and drops they had come to.

From behind the old Motithang Hotel, up above Thimphu on the edge of the jungle, the path led up for two hours until we almost reached a monastery. JJ and I, un-adjusted to the altitude, made a credible effort to keep up with our two Bhutanese guides. At the chorten before the temple we were joined by a dog that refused to leave us. Now we plunged down through the jungle, hit the stream, found the rock steps, and climbed down. The ravine became steeper and steeper forcing us to follow the stream. We literally crawled in the stream under thick bamboo but there were no serious cliffs, and we hit a bigger river which was crossed astride a log. Our faithful canine companion though had to be thrown across by me, and he fell into the river. Luckily he went in near the bank, and one of the Bhutanese managed to haul him out in time before he drowned. The dog wouldn't come near me after that. Sure enough we emerged from the jungle at the king's perimeter fence and startled a young sentry who dropped his old Enfield rifle in shocked surprise. We had to detour up a hill and through more forest to get around the king's log-built palace and came to a village where we were set upon by a small pack of local dogs. The four of us stood back to back fending them off with our sticks until the villagers came to our rescue. A friendly monk gave us a lift back into town and dropped us at the hotel.

But no Harry, and shortly after we arrived back the rest of the expedition arrived from Calcutta. Unfortunately some of the film gear had been off-loaded from the Dornier and had been left behind. Also one of the support trekkers, Jeremy Knight Adams, had missed the flight from London and was also stuck in Calcutta. The film crew wanted to film me giving a report for the Channel Four news programme. They wanted it to sound exciting and positive, but Jeff and I had concluded by now that Harry was dead. We thought he had probably tried to cross the stream and had been carried away by the powerful current. The last thing I wanted to do was hype it up for the media. A couple of hours after that and our Bhutanese hosts threw a cocktail party reception for us. It was so strange – they knew and we knew that Harry was quite possibly dead and yet we all behaved like nothing had happened. There were hot roasted cashew nuts, dried fried liver, spicy sausages, considerable volumes of alcohol, music and laughter, just like my dream. Halfway through the party I went to the toilet in the back of the hotel and as I came back a Bhutanese waiter told me Harry had just arrived. He had been found not far from the king's palace.

He arrived at the party to much cheering, looking somewhat haggard. Maggie and Tan were understandably pretty critical of the fact that he had just gone off on his own leaving the two women to fend for themselves in the jungle. He offered no apology. I think he was still in some sort of shock. Harry's 'rescue' was also a huge relief to the guide who had been with the three of them, a tall lanky Bhutanese called Singey. We were told that Singey was unusual for a Bhutanese and liked bucking the system. He also drank a lot, but then that didn't seem too unusual. It was hinted to us that had Harry not been found alive, Singey would have really been in trouble, and his job and livelihood would have been under severe threat.

The welcome party picked up pace; warm, faltering speeches were made, people hugged each other, we posed with the Bhutanese flag as flashbulbs went off, and Dorji Gyaltshen, Deputy Director of Bhutan Tourism Corporation presented us all with silk scarves. We were told that Jigme Tshultim, the Director, had been unable to attend at the last moment due to a family crisis.

In the morning I was whisked off for an interview for Bhutan Radio, along with Yeshey Wangchuck, the Bhutanese climber who was to join our team. We arrived at a small studio that like all Bhutanese buildings, was decorated inside and out with Buddhist symbols and dragons, painted in bright colours. Their sound equipment consisted of a Sony Walkman and a hand-held microphone. We were interviewed by an Englishwoman, Elizabeth, who was separated from her husband, one of the king's uncles, but who had continued to live in the kingdom. Our film director, Allen Jewhurst, affectionately known as Al, had also put in a formal written request for an interview with the king but after the incident involving Harry I thought there would be little chance of this happening, and so it proved to be.

Thimphu was a small city of some thirty thousand people, and up until I was aged thirteen years (1962) had been connected to India by mule track only. Even visiting Presidents of India had taken six days on horseback to reach Thimphu. In the early sixties the late king had started the process of bringing Bhutan into the twentieth century by building a road from the Indian plains up to his capital. The town itself had wide, tree-lined streets and, like Paro, was dominated by a massive monastery/fortress, the hub of secular and religious power in the kingdom. The least visited of all Himalayan capitals was surrounded on all sides by Himalayan foothills and pine, cedar and rhododendron forests. The valley floor was highly cultivated; houses looking more like Swiss chalets than rough Himalayan farmhouses dotted the landscape.

Although the weather was foul we were thoroughly enjoying ourselves. While Yeshey and I chased around dealing with the finances, and trying to find a way of getting hold of both the missing film equipment and Jeremy, the others wandered around town. They watched some monks dislodging an evil spirit in a shop by chanting and letting off fire-crackers to scare it away. They watched an archery tour-nament, shocked to see a team at either end of the ground taking turns to fire arrows more than a hundred yards down at each others' targets. Some of the contestants, a little the worse for wear, proudly showed off scars on various parts of their bodies where they had been hit by arrows.

In the evening, back at the hotel, I discovered from Al that he wanted to film the annual Thimphu tsechu, or festival, in two days time at the Tashichhodzong, the main monastery/fortress. I pointed out that we would effectively lose days on the mountain, and that delays could affect the trekkers' chances of getting as far as Base Camp. He promised to find a way to pay for any days lost. Apparently Maggie had sanctioned this change to our schedule with Bhutan Tourism without reference to us, and this annoyed me. The climbers were keen to get moving and this would eat into the precious sixty days we had paid so handsomely for. Back in England relations with Maggie had already become a little strained, as she had wanted to charge the trekkers extra for their Bhutan visas, and we had felt this was an extra that was not part of the original price we had quoted them. Now she was taking unilateral decisions that affected us all. At the same time I was very anxious that frictions were kept to a minimum, and in any case although we did not have to wait for Jeremy and the film gear, it would be better to leave Thimphu together. I therefore went to Maggie's room and in the friendliest way possible showed her the film contract which stated that the expedition had the final decision regarding our programme. I had thought that was the end of the matter but no, the very next day the same thing happened again; Maggie sanctioned yet another day's delay without reference to the rest of us, encouraged by Al. This time her action could not be glossed over quite as easily. Monksie and 'Aitch' in particular were really mad, quite rightly so. I called a meeting of all of us and explained the situation; the delays and implications, the pros and cons. We all agreed that Gross Group happiness was all important and that in future Maggie, Al and I would discuss important issues and refer them to the others. Maggie came in for a lot of flak, and privately apologised to me afterwards. Al kept quiet in the background, and his partner in Chameleon Films, our sound recordist Chris Lister, told me privately afterwards that he thought Al should have shouldered more of the blame for the misunderstandings.

That morning Maggie's real motive for coming to Bhutan revealed itself. She came out of a meeting with Jigme Tshultim dancing with joy, claiming to have secured the sole agency for handling Visa entry to

Bhutan from the UK. It was all about money; Maggie wanted to use the expedition as her vehicle to secure the contacts and influence in Bhutan, so that she could start running treks and tours from London. How deeply ingrained with Bhutan Tourism she was I could not be certain.

So while we gazed starry eyed at reincarnate lamas walking the streets, spent our day at the festival watching dancers stamp demons from the earth, and then bounced spellbound across this prayer-flagged land, we were all of us aware of human undercurrents that wriggled to the surface every now and then.

CHAPTER 14

Trouble along the Way

IT STARTED IN JAKAR, the main township in the central region of Bumthang. The main party arrived there the evening before Yeshey and I, because on the drive across, while cautiously driving on a road literally cut out of a sheer rock face, we had rounded a bend to be confronted with a massive rockfall blocking the road. Yeshey and I had then driven back to the last town, Wangdiphodrang, to use the radio there to try and arrange for a lorry to come from the other side of the blockage. The others had scrambled over the landslide and, as luck would have it, found an Indian road gang a few miles up the road. They came and blasted the thousands of tons of rock out of the way and cleared a narrow track for our vehicles. Imagine the surprise for Yeshey and I when we returned to the roadblock, having spent hours trying to use a crackly, antiquated, valve-driven radio to arrange another lorry and hotel accommodation for everyone, only to find there was no one there

Road block on the road from Thimphu to Bumthang.

and the rock slide half blown away. Yeshey and I had chased after the others and arrived at 4.30 a.m., some twenty two hours on the go, only to find there was another delay. The horsemen with sixty six horses had turned up on time two days previously, and when they found we were not there they had returned to their village. We sent a runner to bring them back again.

We had another day to connect with all things Bhutanese. We went to a village festival where a reincarnate lama laid hands on the heads of obeisant men and women. Isn't this what all religions of the world continually strive to do; cleanse people of sin. The Tibetan Buddhist accumulation of 'merit' is a nice twist on the perennial problem – sin if you have to, but build up good karma to negate the sin. Fantastic to see it in progress; behind the village square, out of sight, people were gambling, getting drunk, smoking, and playing games. No doubt like anywhere else in the world, on another level, even more hidden from view, people were having affairs and who knows what else. In the main square the Headman of the village was being ushered into the best seats with his family, while round the back was a man so drunk his embarrassed family were having difficulty trying to revive him. The monks had a tough job.

In the evening we sat round a bonfire and a group of women from the village sang and danced for us. We couldn't figure what had prompted this but whether it was Bhutan Tourism honouring us, or the villagers responding to our friendship, it didn't matter. The fact was their shyness in front of strangers and the high, plaintive, beautifully addictive songs struck the Unforgettable Chord in all of us. The women wore long pleated dresses made of fine patterned, home-woven raw silk or cotton. The dancing seemed simple, until you tried to join in. Yeshey, our Bhutanese climber, turned out to have a classically beautiful girlfriend in Jakar, though he was a married man in Thimphu. Not that we were particularly shocked by this as we had already met one Bhutanese man who had more than one wife. I had been warned by Jigme Tshultim that he drank a lot and was forgetful. I have to say nothing seemed less likely. He was good looking, mature and I never saw him drunk. Many years later though he died from drink and a broken heart. I was told his wife had left him and in later years when he was drunk he did become violent. It seemed inconceivable, poor Yeshey, on the surface everything seemed so in balance. Only once did he show a side to his character that took us all by surprise, but that came later.

That evening really was the first time actually that the whole expedition had been together in one place and free; back at our lodge we carried on partying till the early hours. Lydia and Ginette were both single and most of the male climbers were as well. The evening saw a lot of tomboy flirtation. On the face of it we were just a bunch of mates having a great time, but I think there was an element of the girls sizing up whom they fancied as well. Lydia of course was Monksie's ex-girlfriend and back home some of us had wondered whether this would be a problem. They were both so laidback about it, there really was no issue. Lyd was a rolling stone, up for anything exciting that was going on, loads of guts, uninhibited, ambitious to the extent that she wanted to become famous and make money out of climbing, self focused and pretty much disorganised. She was a great laugh and laughed greatly, so much so you couldn't mistake the fact her genetics were antipodean, and that she was wild and free, with a capital F. You wouldn't call her attractive in the ordinary sense, though there was no denying she had a great body, but her appeal was in her smile and her attitude to life. A rebel and not someone you would get on with if you were conventional. Always hard up for money; she had earned some cash as a still life model. Yet again something she thought was a great laugh, and I bet she had trouble stopping herself from giggling when sitting for her audience of serious minded artists.

That evening she and Ginette raced around like demented schoolgirls, as we listened to solid Western music on a pair of small speakers. The sponsor's Glenfiddich whisky loosened our tongues. I got the feeling that Ginette chatted more with Monksie than anyone, but maybe that was my imagination.

I was thirty seven and still looking, ever more keenly, for my soul mate. As a member of the Bristol climbing scene I had lessened my chances of success in this area considerably. There were very few members of the opposite sex who were capable of putting up with, never mind find interesting, conversations about whether the use of chalk when climbing was morally defensible or not. Climbers talk endlessly about the routes they have done, their grades, particularly the grades, and the near death epics they have survived. When not talking avidly about techniques and moves, they are to be found halfway up this cliff or that cliff. Girls were much more frightening than solid rock. Nevertheless the Bristol climbing scene was never dull. There were always parties to go to; there was always hope.

Over the years I had had a string of girlfriends, some very temporary, but only two or three that were anything like serious. Usually if someone came along who I really thought was great I ended up getting far too keen too quickly and scaring them off. Those I was not so keen on seemed keen on me; I could never get it right. The years drifted by and most of my friends got married and started having kids. I worked hard, I played hard, I had a cool pad in a fashionable part of Bristol, and deep down more than anything I wanted that special bond that only comes from a family around you. In any case the next big scheme was always on the horizon. I daydreamed a lot about lost horizons, and lost opportunities.

I was aware that I thought Ginette was attractive but I was not allowing any flame to be ignited. We were here to climb a mountain and there was so much to think of. I allowed myself an occasional glance in her direction, and I watched and listened, but I entertained no feelings of warmth or desire. Ginette also had something of a reputation, a bit like mine no doubt, of temporary relationships. Back in Bristol she did now have a boyfriend who seemed to be standing the test; a good climbing friend of ours called Julian.

We all of us wondered what would happen next.

The horses turned up the next morning and it was a fine mêlée loading them up. With the ponymen wearing their long machete knifes in wooden scabbards, their circular cane hats and wrap round costumes, and with the horses carrying their loads in wicker baskets, the scene felt positively Mediaeval. Finally we were on our way towards the highest mountain in Bhutan. No one in Thimphu had actually told me how many staff we were being given and I was shocked to discover that we had twelve Bhutanese. This included Yeshey and one other Bhutanese leader, Singye, the nearly disgraced guide, a radio operator for our prehistoric transmitter, two cooks, a Base Camp manager and six camp staff. On top of this there were also the ten ponymen. There were flashes when it felt strange being the 'leader' for such a large group; I told myself just to relax.

It was a long way to the middle of the middle of nowhere. We took ten days to reach the mountain's skirts through appalling weather.

It didn't rain every moment of every day, but when it didn't mist and cloud blocked out the views of the peaks to the north. There were days and days of prime, pristine, muddy jungle. Light bamboo, giant bamboo, giant cedars crazily bedecked with Spanish moss, pine, birch and rhododendron, orchids growing on cliffs beside the path, and meadows of bright flowers some of which we had never seen before. Steve Findlay of the green fingers arrived in camp every day positively chortling to himself.

We met yak herders living in rough, timber shelters on the bare earth, which were full of smoke. Some of the men wore nothing on their feet and their clothes were of coarse, black, homespun yak hair. They grinned at us and we grinned back. Their yak butter, salted, brick tea was as rough as they were, but they liked our roll up tobacco and the Indian cigarettes that I have smoked since that first expedition to Manali. One evening we watched with them as their two largest male yaks fought in the pouring rain by charging at each other head on. Another evening JJ played the mandolin while they played their bamboo pipes and we all shouted and clapped.

We were told not to throw stones into a specific lake they said was holy and to keep in pairs through the forest because of the bears. On the third day in another lake I came upon Steve Monks and Ginette skinny dipping. We laughed and I jokingly took a picture of Ginette as she emerged nude from the still water. Later we discovered that this lake too was regarded as holy, as many years previously a nun had fallen from a cliff into the lake and had been drowned. Luckily our Bhutanese friends were not around at the time of the swimming incident.

By the third day we escaped the dripping forest and climbed past waterfalls, out of a cirque of misty peaks, over a wind-swept pass, heading for the hot springs at Dur Sachu. The path was rocky and halfway up we passed through a strata of rock peppered with rough garnets. I was feeling strong and took a great deal of pleasure from pushing myself as hard as I could.

Sadly, though, Tan MacKay's body did not adjust to the ever increasing altitude and at the end of the first day she had already felt nauseous and had been in tears. She tried to hide it from us but we knew. How she made it to the hot springs I don't know; even the fittest of us were exhausted by the end of that third day. Maggie and Ginette had found her a riding horse, but even so, much of the path was too steep to ride. The fellowship had started to break. Tan had to turn back and Pete Godwin of the *Sunday Times* did too, and so did the weird man the film crew had brought along as their guru. His name was Ole Fink Larsen and he had come supposedly to conduct meaningful, searching interviews with us all. He ran 'self-actualisation' courses in America. I saw him as an amiable enough, unfit freeloader. Peter Godwin on the other hand was a tough young guy, and had just been promoted by the *Sunday Times* to open an office for them in South Africa. He was going through a painful break-up with his girlfriend and his heart was just not in what we were doing. He wanted out.

We all got naked at the sulphurous hot springs. We had crossed a high pass that day and dropped thousands of feet back down into the jungle. The air was humid and hot, a myriad of small brightly coloured birds made a clamour in the dank bushes, and a roaring torrent made us shout to be heard. The boiling hot water turned aching muscles into pleasure. Long after dark we left the hot springs for camp, leaving Pete Godwin and Lydia alone in the simple creeper-covered, timber baths. They had been spending a lot of time together on trek and there was some speculation in the air. Something else though made me jealous that evening; Steve Monks and Ginette casually announced they were going to share a tent together. The way that it had been put across made it sound as though it was a purely innocent thing of friendship only. It was the half expected beginnings and I felt envious. I lay in my sleeping bag that night telling myself that surely she was not about to start a fling with Steve when Julian was our friend and waiting for her in Bristol, and Steve had a serious partner, Jane. In any case I argued, what did it matter to me, and well, if she fancied Monksie that was her business. For all that, I knew my feelings for what they were. I was envious, just very slightly, but I had it in perspective and under control. No problem.

There were other problems to worry about. On Day 2 four of the horses had bolted and some of the luggage got left behind. One of our trekkers, Peter Santamera, spent quite an uncomfortable night sleeping in a down suit Al had lent him as his sleeping bag had been on one of the missing horses. Pete was a wonderful, self-effacing man and accepted the problem stoically. We were lucky in fact the whole of the support team accepted endless changes without thinking to complain about it. Their attitude was 'whatever is good for the climbing team is fine by us'. In fact we were still all revelling in the wildness of the whole experience, the practically unexplored country, the myths and legends of Bhutan, the fact we were being filmed, and that very soon we would be climbing an exceedingly difficult mountain. We had a few photos of the peak given to us by Michael Ward, the expedition doctor for the '53 Everest expedition, who had been a heart specialist looking after the late king. He had been given permission by the king to trek into Lunana and had taken pictures of Gangkar Punsum from a trekking peak, I think, he and his friend had climbed.

The horses caught up, but then at the hot springs, where the Bhutanese had arranged in advance a change over from horses to yaks, Yeshey came to me and told me there were only forty one yaks. Not a sufficient number to carry all our loads to Base Camp. Equipment and food was again going to be left behind, to be brought up later, and we then had to reorganise the loads. There was general desire in any case for a rest day. It meant that there was time enough then for Ole to work his magic interviews. A minor row had been brewing about this because Al Jewhurst, the film director, had wanted to bring Ole further on, but I could see the Bhutanese did not like this idea. From their standpoint it made sense for Ole to go back with the horses. Al, the ultimate juggler of situations, eventually agreed.

Two days out from the hot springs, breakfast consisted of a bit of asparagus, a small portion of porridge, and some mouldy bread. Naturally there were complaints and a few people were beginning to ask searching questions about the seeming lack of staple foods. Yeshey came to me and confessed that they had practically run out of a few essential items and suggested we stayed put for another day. He told me he had already sent fourteen yaks back to the hot springs to fetch food that had been left behind. He thought also that something had gone wrong with the arrangements he had said he had made for more yaks. By now I had come to realise that if there was a problem the Bhutanese kept it to themselves. They also didn't like replying to anything in the negative. If I asked them a question to which the truthful answer was something they thought I wouldn't want to hear, they would evade a direct answer. So it was now; hanged if I could discover why the food had been left behind. I think it was a case of sheer bad organisation; probably it was not clear enough who was supposed to make the decisions, so nobody did.

That evening our Bhutanese friends gave us two bottles of Bhutanese brandy to make up for the fact we were about to lose another day. We talked very merrily into the evening and as it turned out finally I was left alone with Ginette. My diary records that we talked about love, that it was a tantalising conversation of things unsaid. I remember fondly that we hugged each other, and she told me she was not having an affair with Monksie. Under the sweet beguiling innocence of a pure friendship there was no denying I had started to want physical contact as well. I had trouble sleeping that night.

We were now only two days from Base Camp but the weather was foul. The campsites were all mud and yak shit. At the last pair of yak herder huts before Base Camp we were getting ready to leave when someone ran up and said "Hey Steve there's a fight going on." We raced round the back of one of the huts and two of the yak men were shouting full bore at each other. Their friends were trying to calm the situation, and I think because we had arrived, one of them tried to make himself look big by pulling his sword out. Then they really were going to land blows and it took several of our staff to separate them. In the way things are in Bhutan we never did find out the reasons that lay behind the violence.

Also during the day approaching this last camp I nearly got trampled to death by a group of yaks on a narrow mountain path. They were ahead of me and something spooked them. They simply turned round and charged. I had a split second not to believe what was happening, and it was damn lucky that there was a steep bank to scramble up as they thundered beneath me.

On the last day, after the fight, we set off in still mist, and as the day wore on the weather improved fractionally. We watched lammergeiers wheel in the mountain currents, caught glimpses of shy blood pheasants amongst the rhododendron bushes, and we could now see up the mammoth Mangde Chu valley we were essentially traversing along, but still Gangkar Punsum hid herself from view.

Just before lunch a few of us sat down for a rest and sitting down behind Lydia I tipped her hat off with the point of my umbrella, so she playfully fought with me. Ginette joined in, Lyd dropped out and I was left wrestling with Ginette. We rolled around and I bit her neck. We stopped and she said, "I bet I can pin you down." We started again and I did gain control, rolled over exhausted and she then pinned me down. The altitude left us gasping for air, but I felt warm and happy to be fighting her. We got up and brushed each other down. Lydia looked on smiling.

The path had disappeared now, the land belonged to nature, and to the minute as we approached the final pass the cloud shredded from our peak. 'Here I am' she seemed to say 'look how beautiful I am. Do you think your spirit is pure enough to win me as your prize?' Suddenly it seemed a happy friendly place to be, just because the sun was shining, and because the mountain was there to gaze at in all her power. Down below the pass lay an emerald lake. This is where the Japanese and the Austrians had had their bases. It seemed too far from the base of the mountain for our liking. I walked down the final five hundred foot slope to Base Camp with Maggie. We hadn't really had more than brief conversations for days, and now she talked about her husband, her friendship with Doug Scott, and her parents. I think we were both anxious to repair any lingering damage caused by the stresses and strains in the early days, and we talked freely and openly. She shared with me the grief of her mother's death, and my suspicions of her inner motives fell away and I saw her as a caring woman. We are all human when it comes down to it.

We worked out that the trekkers could afford to spend two days at

Base with us and still stand a chance of catching their flights home. For three weeks we had shared tents, eaten all our meals together, trekked paths that few white man had ever seen before, watched from our Western standpoint this fairytale kingdom, been exhausted and soaked to the skin together, and talked almost non stop about ourselves, our lives and our problems. We had grown so close to all of them. There was the laid-back American emergency hospital doctor who was JJ's landlord, seemingly the least complicated person. There was lanky, long haired Brian who walked the whole way in trainers, who ran a large garden centre but ought to have been living in a hippy commune. Then there was the techy computer whiz kid marathon runner from Swindon, the double barrelled property developer with a habit of missing flights, a larger than life businessman who followed cricket all round the world, the mild mannered marine engineer, and the Asiatic looking body scanner technician who had got lost in the jungle at the start. There was not one who grated on anyone else's nerves, no one who could not hack it when the going got tough, no one who whinged and whined. The thing was they had all been rooting for us not knowing what we were facing. Then arriving at Base Camp each had seen the reality of the South West Ridge through the film cameraman's 600mm lens. Their quiet looks, their sad expressions told us our new found family was worried for our safety.

Most wanted to carry loads for us through the glacier to an Advance Base Camp just to help in any way they could. The route was a broken ankle waiting to happen, across a slag heap of a moraine-strewn glacier. I made my first carry on the second day and took nine hours returning utterly exhausted, bringing with me a thumping headache. Only Harry McAulay waited for me, encouraging me on. In camp I crawled into my sleeping bag and an hour later someone shouted the dinner call. I could hardly stand the thought of our 'last supper' with the trekkers; I was so dead beat, and it would be down to me to make an emotion-fuelled speech. At the end of the meal, when it had all gone quiet, I was still not 'with it' enough to find the right words. Instead John Knowles, the elder statesman of the trekking group, stood up and made an impassioned speech, saying how this had been the best thing he had done in his life, and thanked Maggie and I for putting it all together. His emotion stirred us all and I then stood up and said I would try to get them all to cry but that I might break down first, that it would seem incredibly strange to be without them, and all we would have left was the film crew, which brought a few laughs. Then spontaneously everyone took turns in saying his or her bit, with the Glenfiddich, Hennesey and

Makers Mark going round liberally. The stereo was put on and I went round serving coffee feeling so warm towards everyone. I sat down and Maggie behind me leant forward and started kissing me. God it felt good. It was not too hard and urgent, just fabulously erotic, and we were not going to stop until we had had enough. Lovely tonguing, licking each others lips and moaning, not that anyone could hear, they were cheering too loudly. We broke and she said in my ear, "I've been saving you up till last." She sat in front of me then and I wrapped my arms round her. John Knowles was in a similar reverse position with Lydia, Peter MacPherson behind her. Ginette was sitting on Jeremy's lap and we became a singing swaying bunch of pissed people singing song after song after song. I remember Harry Jensen was in one corner, his eyes like an owl, blinking. Al was in his onepiece, red down suit and came out with all kinds of east end of London, Cockney rhymes. 'Lucy Grace' by William Wordsworth was recited by John Knowles, there came Bhutanese songs from Yeshey and Singey, solos by the Yak herders, and all the kitchen staff joined in with everything, and everyone laughed non-stop. Lyd went round hugging all the trekkers, and we sang and we sang. Whole eras of pop, U.S. songs, children's songs, old favourites and even one rude song, 'Swing Low, Sweet Chariot' with all the hand gestures, which reduced the Bhutanese to hysterics. This was on the floor of the mess tent with it snowing outside, and as we did not want to waste batteries, illumination was one candle and a couple of weak fluorescent mini tubes. Someone had picked some wild cannabis along the path, dried the leaves, and joints of grass were rolled in air mail paper. People lay in heaps. Steve Findlay was waking and sleeping and playing the harmonica. We sang anything we could think of and some things several times. The energy waxed and waned but no one was going to be the first to leave. Peter MacPherson by the end was nibbling Lydia behind John Knowles. We sang for five hours non stop, and drunk we staggered still singing through the snow to our tents. It was the best evening I have ever had, and how I wished there was some way I could have slept with Maggie. I could have turfed Yeshey out, as she was sharing with him, but lacked the nerve. Lying in my tent how easily thoughts of Maggie eclipsed Ginette. Lust knocks reason into touch for me every time. She had asked when I would be back in Thimphu and I wondered about suggesting we take a hotel room together, but pulled back from asking. I dreamt in the night that I was with her in bed, and that I confessed to her that I had not fully trusted her back in England. In the morning I used the dream to make the confession a reality.

CHAPTER 15

A Beginning

THAT MORNING THERE WERE TEARS AS OUR FRIENDS LEFT. I am sure they were imagining that they would not see some of us again. We watched them as they disappeared into the filthy weather that engulfed the pass.

We all now just wanted to climb, but unfortunately the next two days brought serious practical problems we had just not expected. In England we had agreed with the film company that the crew would be based at Base Camp, and if the route in the early stages was easy then we might take them as far as Camp 1 but that thereafter we would do the filming ourselves. We had after all filmed on the previous two expeditions. The problem was that because Base was so far from the mountain the film crew wanted to place themselves at Advance Base, and we thought we just didn't have enough cooking gas for them as well. That seemed bad enough but then on the second afternoon I got back to camp, after carrying a load, and was told that no lunch had been served, and no tea produced. A truly unholy row broke out with Al Jewhurst ripping into Yeshey telling him that the camp staff were useless and ought to be changed. How the hell that was going to happen when we were ten days' hard walking from the nearest road I don't know. It was a piece of untypical white man's arrogance and it took a bit of swift panic diplomacy to defuse an angry scene. Then we were told that the potatoes had run out, and the biscuits, and slowly but surely the real truth emerged. Yeshey then finally, shamefacedly, admitted to us that he had understood from the Ministry that he only had to provide food to Base Camp not at Base Camp. The printed book of Rules and Regulations written and produced by the Ministry, which I then read out, could not have been clearer. They were supposed to cater for Base Camp meals, while we were only expected to provide high altitude food on the mountain. At this Lydia and Peter Mac Pherson exploded outside the mess tent, though of course the Bhutanese could hear every word, shouting that it was a deliberate rip off and a con by the Ministry. Poor Yeshey bore the brunt of this and he repeatedly apologised for the mistakes at Head Office. I asked him to do a thorough stock take, and in fact the result was nothing like as bad as we feared.

We were not going to starve but the 'goodies' were going to run out pretty quickly. Yeshey agreed to order two weeks' more food for six people by radio; it would take at least two weeks to arrive and would make up the shortfall. He also told us that there was already seven days' food on its way to us, sufficient for all of us for the return journey. Clearly they had already concluded they had messed up big time. Then without consultation, someone, whether it was the cook or Yeshey or both I couldn't say, decided to slaughter a yak to supplement the food. Its severed head was placed on top of the kitchen tent rock. Not a Buddhist thing to do! The wrangling went on most of an afternoon and in the course of it I went to get Monksie from his tent to get him involved in the food quantities as he was the Food Officer. When I opened the tent Ginette was just wearing knickers and a T shirt and Monksie was stripped to the waist. It was an awkward moment, and difficult to sound relaxed and as if nothing was happening there. It had been a stressful, fractious day with hot tempers, a measure of back biting, and anyone's back would do, including mine for being squeamish about not wanting to eat the slaughtered yak meat. Still it seemed the Bhutanese were taking it on the chin and were prepared to rectify the problem, though there were those of us who were, frankly, sceptical of the new made promises.

Finally we went to bed and in the dead of night I woke up to the unmistakable sounds of Ginette and Monksie making love in the next tent. I lay there feeling many bad things about this. Monksie had a girl-friend back in Bristol who had only just followed him over from Australia, and Ginette had Jules. Really it had been clear from the outset that Steve was out to seduce Ginette and hang the rest.

We all loved Steve for his permanent zest for life, with his famous infectious grin. Monksie was the perfect male climbing specimen; massive power to weight ratio, and instantly likeable personality. It was difficult for him to go wrong frankly. He was now widely acclaimed as the best rock-climber in Australia, and lived a life we were all envious of. He guided in the summer in the Alps and in the winter returned to Oz to spend most of his time rock-climbing and exploring. The innocence of his youth had worn off, however, and a harder edge was apparent on this trip. Nevertheless the rebel's grin was as convincing as ever.

Who was I to moralise anyway. I was as ready as he was to ignore our friend in Bristol, Jules. I had hoped that Monksie would stand aside and let me pursue Ginette. He was aware of my own confused feelings towards her, and as a close friend he knew how desperate I was to find a partner.

I opened the snow valance window and looked out. It was a clear night and virgin Gangkar Punsum shone in the starlight. A silly thought entered my mind; how could we succeed on something so perfect when we were so full of imperfections ourselves?

The next morning as I sat on a rock writing my diary Lydia came up to me and with a wide grin on her face asked if I was going to go to Bangkok after the trip. It was none too subtle a way of trying to make light of the situation to cheer me up. Monksie also sauntered over and conversationally said, "Christ, it was freezing last night." Unfortunately I had not the wit to reply, "Yes, if you weren't in your sleeping bag." At breakfast Ginette was the last to arrive, and when she left I looked at her, then at Lyd who gave me a significant smile and raised her eyebrows. It said everything.

People started to depart to take loads and occupy Advance Base. I stayed behind to radio Thimphu for the food. Tobgay, the radio operator, and some of the staff got the generator going and then strung large loops of copper wire around the hillside. There was also an aerial on top of a tall pole, and soon morse code was being tapped out from inside the wigwam tent that housed the primitive radio. It took half an hour to receive a reply and then Tobgay was able to connect me to the Ministry by voice mike. I cast no blame, just said I understood there had been a miscalculation and was promised food supplies within eight or nine days. I left to follow the others.

In the pursuit of the truth of what happened on the expedition I believe I have made it sound like the whole thing was centred on relationships, but this is not close to the mark. We had our problems but they were the sub strata, the behind the scene desires and stresses. We had come to climb the mountain and for all that had happened we were using our combined experience now to figure a route, and get what we needed to the right place in the right order. Mainly we spent our time discussing the pros and cons of the various possible routes to gain the main ridge to the summit. We were walking, climbing and living in amongst mountains that were untouched, unspoilt, and where only wild animals and eagles had previously come and gone. We were psyched up for the climb; Ginette and Steve was a minor side show.

We were all in awe of the mountain. One morning I decided to get up pre dawn to watch the sunrise and when I emerged as quietly as I could, so as not to disturb any of the others, I found to my surprise that Steve Findlay and Capt Kathmandu were already ahead of me. It was bitterly cold but the solar light show was well worth numbed hands and frozen eyelashes.

The climbing started. It took us all of the next week to establish Camp 1, only two thousand feet above us. The climbing was hard and dangerous, and the route the kind of thing that I had only experienced previously in nightmares. Steve Findlay led some heart-in-the-mouth mixed ground, which only years of blind trust in your partner enabled you to partially dispel the desire to give up and go down. The man had nerves of steel. When following his boldest lead I was certain I was going to fall off, sparks flew from my crampons and it is the one time in my life where heart and lungs practically blew to pieces. Finally we came to a section of steep or vertical granite that already had one strand of frayed and faded Japanese fixed rope, and a newer Austrian rope. After pulling on the latter with all his strength Steve clipped his jumar on the rope and clamped his way up the rope out of sight, not knowing what the rope was fixed to, or what state it was in. Had the rope broken there was nothing to stop a fall to the glacier two thousand feet below.

Then the weather broke and we retreated to Base Camp to rest, regain strength and to avoid consuming valuable high altitude food and cooking gas. The promised yaks had not arrived and even basic food-stuffs were getting low. Dossing around in a storm becomes an artform. I actually like it; the howling wind, the deep drumming of rip-stop nylon, reading books, playing Scrabble, rapping about this and that, hunkered up in the cosy confines of a four season down sleeping bag. We invented our own hybrid game of solo whist which we played for small stakes, a rupee a point it was. Yeshey on the other hand, along with most of the Bhutanese staff, had their own card school going, the difference being that they gambled heavily, apparently for serious stakes. Yeshey lost all his cash and the wages he was due to be paid after the expedition. Of course, we never found this out until years later. I would normally be suspicious of the truth of a story like this, however, I have heard the same tale from several Bhutanese friends over the years. We often watched with great amusement as their school became heated and cards slammed down on the table. There was great deal of laughter too, and at the time I don't think any of us realised that the stakes were that serious.

We talked and laughed a great deal, aided by whisky in the evenings and the last joint of grass. It is incredible to think that there were no serious personality clashes in the close confines of our small society. The reason was that we were high on adrenalin. We were enjoying the climb and the prospects were good. We had Camp 1 in place, we were all fit and well, and we still had time to reach that purer plane at the top of the mountain. The film crew had also turned out to be great company. Always the danger of a clique forming, of an us and them thing, but it never happened. They had their own tents but there the division finished. They joined in with everything, and could spout epic yarns as well as we could. Al was the extrovert crafty cockney and their boss in all but name. In theory Chris Lister, his fellow director at Chameleon Films, and soundman, had an equal say but he was an altogether quieter person. They had brought along a young lad as gofer, Mark, who couldn't believe his luck to be on the trip in the first place. Lastly there was Peter McPherson who was the freelance adventure cameraman. The Chameleon guys talked about Peter behind his back, jokingly saying he was a bit too 'proper' for their liking, and they joked that the only things he slept with were his fifty thousand pounds worth of cameras and lenses. True he never let them out of his sight, and true he had turned an Englishman's blind eye to the advances on his honour by Lydia, who fancied him like mad. Not only was Peter being paid as cameraman he was also being paid a hire fee for all his camera equipment. We gathered he had it well-insured.

Every day we expected the yaks to arrive and they did not. Yeshey told me that the two lots of supplies were now going to arrive together; he had heard news of its progress on the radio. I suspected that again the whole truth was being hidden from me, but the detail didn't matter. At least the yaks were on the way. The yaks still did not arrive and the weather slowly improved over four idle days.

On the second day Yeshey took me to one side and said he had decided not to carry on climbing. He said he felt his duty was to organise the new supplies that were coming, and in any case he did not like our high altitude food. It took me so by surprise all I could say to him was that I would think about it. Certainly Harry had told me he thought he was lazy, and so had Ginette, but I had written this off as the sort of minor complaining that you get from time to time on an expedition. Surely it was to be expected that he wouldn't necessarily mesh that easily with a bunch of British climbers.

But why had he taken this decision? It was not through lack of climbing skill. He had climbed with us on the day when Steve Findlay had led the hardest pitches, and he had followed without an expletive, or without his eyes popping out of his head. We had been impressed; to be so cool on such steep ground meant we had a valuable companion, not an encumbrance. He was supposed to be Bhutan's best climber, trained in Japan, had a house full of climbing photos, and four expeditions in Bhutan to his credit. He had met Reinhold Messner. Here was an incredible opportunity for him to climb Bhutan's highest mountain and become a national hero. What was it? Was it the stresses of the major foul ups with supplies? Could have been – he certainly had to bear the brunt of the anger; perhaps he felt he was not entirely welcome. By nature he was a mild mannered, almost shy man. Civilised, not strong and aggressive and maybe he was hiding feelings deep inside. In any case by not climbing with us he would lay himself open to all sorts of criticism when he got back to Thimphu. Being human maybe the temptations of friends, gambling and Bhutanese food at Base Camp was inflaming that old climbers' weakness – the 'stay in the café' syndrome. Maybe it was fear of the mountain. Maybe even there was a more powerful internal struggle beneath his impassive, urbane surface. He was a product of the new generation of Bhutanese who were shyly welcoming the outside. In a country as traditional as Bhutan he was flying in the face of their beliefs. The mountains were thought of as gods, beings who affected the weather, the health of people and animals, who if angered could bring on calamity and bad fortune. Yet here he was climbing them. All Bhutanese in some degree or other, believe in fateful powers, dharma and destiny, and not without reason. There are

Yeshey Wangchuck.

many strange, unexplainable forces at work in the kingdom. Perhaps Yeshey was fighting a struggle between wanting to climb and not wanting to anger the gods.

Whatever was the reigning force in his decision to quit I was not going to accept it so easily. The next day I set up a meeting and gave it the full throttle persuasion technique. I actually felt the core of the problem was a fear on his part that he was not liked, and sought to make him believe we all really wanted him to stay and be the first Bhutanese to climb their highest mountain. I promised that we would bring Bhutanese food with us just for him. I apologised for the hostility directed at him because of the supplies, and told him I did not think it was his fault. I reasoned, cajoled and pleaded with him as a friend. He agreed to stay but I could see this was probably because he did not want to give me a negative answer. My show of friendship had not rekindled a fire of ambition, but I hoped that as we got going again he would dispel his worries whatever they were, and come to the top with us.

All this provoked a row with Lydia who thought I should have left him alone to make his own decision. I thought otherwise, and recorded in my diary angrily that I thought she had about as many brain cells as a jellyfish. In the event, after the yaks failed to arrive, Yeshey came again to me and said he must go with Goppa to look for them. He promised to return and to climb with us. I watched them heading towards the now snow-covered pass with misgivings for his return.

In actual fact what then happened was that as Yeshey and Goppa started to cross the pass they encountered deep snow, got lost, darkness fell and they barely survived the night by clinging to each other for warmth under a rock. They carried on the next day and quite what happened next is not clear. Certainly news somehow filtered back to the capital over the following weeks that they had died. Thimphu had been full of this rumour apparently. Yeshey and Goppa did escape and trekked all the way back to civilisation. Upon reaching the capital they told their story to the Ministry and gave the impression to the decision-makers that the expedition was cut off by snowed-up passes. It was to have far reaching implications at the end of our climb.

CHAPTER 16

The Climbing

GANGKAR PUNSUM AT LAST DEFEATED THE STORM, and was revealed again painted a fresh coat of pure matt white. We returned in dribs and drabs to Advance Base and by the time I got there Captain Kathmandu and Monksie were already perched at Camp 1. That first night at ABC a deafening 'surroundasound' avalanche came down the gully the Japanese had taken as their route. It slammed into the glacier half a mile away, making our tents shake, and then two days later a second one followed the first, exactly at the time that we would have been in the gully. We felt somewhat vindicated that we had chosen our own line.

A little over one thousand five hundred feet above Camp 1 was the Snow Dome, a sort of small summit on the other side of which was a razor ridge about half a mile long. Cloud plumes boomed off its southern side formed by the pressure drop as the prevailing winter wind from the Tibetan plateau hit its North Face. It looked like the undulating back of a dinosaur, and was heavily corniced. On the far side the arrow straight granite ridge rocketing to the summit waited, seemingly the only way to go. From the top of the snow dome, just looking at the 'Dinosaur' was ten times more frightening than contemplating the worst ride at Alton Towers, where at least human design ensured you got off the other end giggling. There were no such guarantees with Gangkar Punsum.

We were racing against time now; we had paid for just sixty days in Bhutan, and food was running out, but we had enough of both if only the weather would hold. As we climbed higher trying to get Camp 2 in at the other end of the 'Dinosaur', the skies remained clear but the mountain conjured another weapon to attack us with, the wind. Time and again we ventured out onto the steep fragile back of the 'Dinosaur' while non-stop ice blasts sought to freeze us or throw us into space. We managed slowly to creep along its undulating back, fixing ropes which blew out in arching loops. It took several teeth-in-the-wind, beards-full-of-ice attempts over many days but finally Monksie and Ginette got there. Capt. Kathmandu and I were right behind them and next to a small col, up against the ridge leading on up above to the summit, we dug out a shelf in the only place possible to pitch our small tent. Monksie and Ginette retreated to rest, leaving JJ and I to take a turn up front, but the mountain took a very dim view of this and increased the wind speed to hurricane force. We had no sooner cooked our evening meal inside the tent when the howling banshees arrived. Their mournful screaming did not stop for a second for thirty six hours. Luckily for us we had dug right in behind a rock outcrop into a snow mushroom otherwise we would not have survived.

All we had were some noodles, mash, soup and a few fig cakes which we reckoned we could eke out on starvation rations for three days. The tent was small, with no bell end for cooking, so that had to be done inside. With the door closed the cooker consumed the oxygen and gave us headaches, but if we opened the door a vicious wind blew ice particles in like angry bees. We ate a lot of Paracetamol. We read a book torn in half, played some cards and had shouted conversations. Capt. K had a very poor view of American politicians. During the day reality was bearable but when night came we got a taste of what madness would have been like had we got stuck there. For me sleep wasn't sleep, it was a series of violent nightmares, in which it seemed that death lay, unless I could escape the evil pursuing me. I would find myself wrenching myself awake, only to slip back again in exhaustion to the horrors that lurked in unfinished dreams that started again where I had left off. I could imagine that if you spent too long up here and ran out of food, weakness would take over and this truly evil twilight zone would become inescapable. When we were on the approach trek, news had come through on a short wave radio that a friend of ours, Al Rouse, had died on K2, trapped in a storm at Camp 6. What we were experiencing must have been a fraction of what Al would have suffered. It wasn't encouraging.

It was very cold and uncomfortable, and the tent was a well-made bag of constantly loud, thrumming, banging fabric. Although my eternal optimism told me that everything would be alright, because it always had been in my life until now, I knew that the living lay at the other end of the 'Dinosaur' and that whatever happened we would have to try to get back across it, at some point. I kept telling myself that the wind would eventually die, but it became easy to believe as the hours dragged on that maybe the jetstream winds were not going to stop until next spring.

The 'Dinosaur' ridge.

We waited. The tent was not big enough to sit up properly. We took detailed care of our space and eked out the time. We had not quite descended to taking our craps inside the tent. We went out into the maelstrom and did it right outside the door, as fast as we could. We had a snow shovel with us and the offending waste was picked up each time and thrown into the gully where the hurricane blasted the turds into the sky; quite an amusing sight to watch actually.

On the second night, in unguarded moments I allowed thoughts to surface that I might not be strong enough for a summit bid. Strange really that we were still thinking it could be possible. We had still not given up hope. Logically I felt that if the weather did eventually clear it would be better to have the fresher, stronger climbers at Camp 2. In any case we had to go back across the 'Dinosaur' for food. Jeff, however, had decided he was not going to go down, not going to give up his chance at the top, not going to give up pole position. We knew whoever went to the summit would have to descend from Camp 2 on 28th October, to allow enough time for us all to start the hike out on 3rd November from Base. It was now the 20th. We still had a week.

Two mornings after the start of the hurricane, suddenly there was a change in the howling noise and within an hour the wind halved in strength. That was it, we were out of there. JJ was so laid-back that packing was always a boring chore, and he was late as usual getting started. It took three hours for the half mile along the Dinosaur ridge. At the beginning I was nervous and clumsy, fearful of every step, but by the time I reached the Snow Dome I was actually enjoying myself again, probably because the fear had come under control. JJ arrived, beard encased in icicles, and said, "I really don't know whether I can make it back again Steve." I knew what he meant; it would mean going back into the wind. Trouble was he had only come to pick up the food from a dump at the Snow Dome. His sleeping bag and personal gear were back at Camp 2. He had to go back. I wished him luck, gave him a hug and left; about ten minutes later the wind miraculously died right away.

When I got down to Camp 1 Monksie and Ginette, because of the drop in the wind, were packing up their dome tent and had decided to make a late dash for Camp 2. As they feverishly packed they gave a disjointed, strange story of how the yaks had not got through because of the snow on the pass, how Yeshey and Goppa had taken five days to reach the hot springs, wading through waist deep snow, how four yak men had got to Base Camp with meagre supplies, how the staff were leaving in five days, and how there had been talk of helicoptering us out.

In the afternoon Steve Findlay and Lydia arrived from Advance Base with another dome tent, Mars Bars, high altitude food and some film gear for Al who, incredibly, was half an hour behind them.

He was utterly all in and suffering from a blinding headache, dressed in the one-piece red down suit given to him by the late Don Whillans. We often joked about the fact that Al's gear was all left overs from dead climbers; Pete Boardman's gloves, Joe Tasker's axe, Whillans's suit. It had all been donated to him on various expeditions over the years. Even one of his Bolex autoload cameras had been used to shoot the summit pictures on Kongur, when Al Rouse and others had made the first ascent. In any case Al said it was the hardest thing he had ever done, and now his ambition was to get to the Snow Dome to film us climbing along the 'Dinosaur'.

With them came more conflicting rumours about what was happening down at Base Camp. They told us that the cook, Phuntso, had been over to ABC with a note from Chris Lister telling the story of the yaks. Phuntso had brought over the first mail we had received since the beginning of the expedition, which had taken six weeks to reach us. He picked up Yeshey's abandoned climbing gear and went back to Base. Chris himself had come across the following day, to ABC, to clarify things, and to try and make contact with us on the mountain, using the walkie-talkies. However, with no clear line of sight between ABC and Camp 1 the radios did not work, so Harry had gone back down to Base to try to contact us from there. He had managed to speak to Ginette and Monksie and had said that the radio operator had been persuaded to stay and that he was trying to find out what was happening with the helicopters. He wasn't sure whether the rest of the staff were going to stay or not. I knew that the Mountaineering Rules and Regulations stated clearly that helicopters would only be used by agreement between the expedition Leader and Thimphu, and so far I had not been consulted. The decision by the authorities to use helicopters had been taken because Yeshey had convinced them that yaks would be unable to reach us. The truth was that we liked the idea of getting out by helicopter but didn't want to pay for it. No one had mentioned payment and we imagined that the Bhutanese, having taken the decision, were going to pay. At the same time we understood that the staff were expected to walk out. How they were going to do this no one seemed to know, but we supposed it was a Thimphu cost cutting exercise. Certainly the tents and gear could be left behind, and there was just enough room for a few men to sleep in the rough yak huts we had seen on the way up. This no doubt is what the staff were expected to do. When we did meet up with them at Base they accepted the situation without a murmur of protest, but we knew and they knew that they were going to be treated to the rough end of the stick.

The next day Al and I took a load of things we knew the climbers needed for the summit bid; mainly fixing ropes, but also a film camera. Just below the Snow Dome we had previously discovered a practically buried tent abandoned by the Austrians, and by the time we reached it Al couldn't take another step forward and left me to carry on. The temptation to dump my load at the top of the Snow Dome was nigh on irresistible, but I knew they wanted the rope badly. It was getting late in the day to reach Camp 2 and get back before night closed in, so I decided that I would stop and turn around no later than 2.30 p.m. In fact I arrived at Camp 2 at 3.00 p.m. anxious now to just dump the rope and head back. Their plan was to avoid the granite arêtes of the ridge by dropping down onto the face, traversing out on steep ice, to four steep snowfields that looked like they would connect and lead to the summit. JJ and I had had this discussion; he preferred the granite rock-climbing, but I was relieved he had been overruled; the granite ridge looked desperately hard climbing for this altitude. They were going to have a day's rest and try and fix rope on the ice traverse, then 'go for it' in a non stop push to the summit, bivouacking if necessary.

I knew in those few minutes that my chances of the summit were slipping away, and they knew it too. I wished them luck and take care, Lydia kissed me, Steve Findlay leant out of their tent and shook my hand. They all looked fit and strong and full of optimism. I turned and fled at snail's pace back along the 'Dinosaur'. Past a spot where a cornice the size of a double-decker bus had calved off right next to Monksie; his bootprint was right there six inches from the fracture line. Over a series of cornices that should have fallen off with me on top of them but didn't and through the worst of it to watch the most spectacular sunset I have ever seen. There were seas of clouds, coloured pink and purple with the sun sinking into them in a blaze of orange. That evening Al cooked a wonderful round of soups and coffee. I ate chocolate, a veggie burger, goulash and mash. It was the end of another nine hour day of focus and extreme fatigue, but after a few hours sleep I woke and could not stop thinking about the decision not to try for the summit. The arguments went round and round on an endless loop of un-resolved logic. Was I strong enough? Yes, if the weather held fine. Was I as strong as the others? Probably not, could be I'd be a hindrance, especially as we would be carrying big loads. Would the weather hold for three or four days from Camp 2 to the top? I doubted it. The risk for me personally was way beyond reasonable limits. It would not be fair on my parents and my sister to take such a risk, better I pull back and let stronger people do it, and help them. Wouldn't people say I was scared? Yes, probably. Wasn't I missing the chance of a lifetime? Yes, undoubtedly. Missing also a chance to beat my altitude record on Nun of 23,410ft, and missing the view into Tibet and missing doing the summit filming. But the final conclusion was that it was way beyond my reasonable limits. My success was in putting the trip together. I would think and think for what seemed hours, piling all the pro arguments onto one side of the scales and all the con arguments onto the other side. Just when I thought I had reached the correct conclusion the logic loop would start at the beginning, and I would change my mind. It was terrible, one minute I was going to go back up, the next I had decided to stay in support.

In the early hours the wind picked up again threatening to wreck the tent. It continued to blow hard all day. The immensely frustrating thing was that every day there was not a cloud in the sky, and by midday the temperatures inside the tent were devastating, but the jetstream made climbing impossible and the wind chill once outside numbed any exposed flesh in minutes. Every evening we had tried to contact Base by radio and that night we finally got through on the walkie-talkie. We were told we were going to be helicoptered out, but that we needed to give five days' notice. I told Harry the third of November was the likely date. Through the static I understood the gist of what was coming through. Pete, Chris and Mark were going to be airlifted the next day, and there had already been food drops.

Al and I were frankly so bored of being in the tent by now we said to each other that whatever the weather we would get fully kitted out and struggle up to the Snow Dome. The wind, however, took no notice of our resolve and continued to try to blow the house down. We got dressed into everything we could think of, stepped outside and stepped back in again. It was simply crazy trying to move in such wind. We spent hours talking about our lives, drinking brews, and playing cards. Al was an East End kid. His old man had had a scaffolding business and his uncle had been killed in a fall, so Al was not allowed to enter the firm. As a young lad he had landed a job as a 'runner' at Shepperton Studios, which eventually led to film editing. At twenty one he had found himself out of work and took to jobbing building and petty crime. We hit human sub strata now, skeletons in the closet stuff, all the raw material of life. I told him how my brother had committed suicide, how it had come about, and the devastation that that had caused in our family and to our friends. How as a young man of nineteen I had so nearly become involved in drug dealing, and how love of my parents and respect for them had brought me back from living a life as a hippy in Morocco. Al too had escaped crime and got back into film editing, and then came a move to Yorkshire TV. He left there to make his first independent film about a British winter attempt on K2. He had gone on to build up a strong independent film company, specialising in adventure films, and he owned a sound effects company, and various properties that he let out. He had bought his parents a house, and had a smart bachelor pad in Leeds.

Around one o'clock we heard a female voice outside the tent. We both jumped upright. We both instantly imagined that there must have been a tragedy for Lydia to be back at Camp 1. But no, she recounted how they had decided to call off the attempt. The winds were just too high. JJ and Monksie had tried to traverse across the ice to the snow fields and had taken four hours to go two hundred and fifty feet, and had returned with frost nip in their fingers. Finders was next to arrive, Monksie, JJ late starting as usual, and lastly Ginette who was suffering from stomach trouble. They all looked spent and told of a desperate time coming across the 'Dinosaur' in the high winds. All were united in the conviction that it was out of the question in the winds and the cold. The conclusion was that the jetstream was early that year, and that really we were lucky to have got out of there alive. By about 3.30 p.m. they had all gone on down to ABC, and the wind was only moderate. Al and I had decided to stay. There was a valuable Scoopic camera in the wrecked Austrian tent and Al wanted to get it, and still hankered after filming some shots of the 'Dinosaur' from the Snow Dome. He couldn't stay on his own, so I said I'd stay. I very nearly took a sleeping pill and was glad I didn't.

CHAPTER 17

Rejection

ABOUT THREE IN THE MORNING I woke to find Al pushing at the wall of the tent which was collapsing on top of us. The wind had turned and was here again with the banshees, hosing eighty mile an hour mayhem at our technological tent. Part of the fly had come off, and would rip right off, unless we kept the tent upright. We piled everything we could against the windward side and then sat with our backs to the wall. It was like hanging onto a pneumatic drill gone loco. We were shaken like rag dolls as we fought to stay upright. So lucky for us that the day before, during lulls in the wind, we had gone round the whole tent checking and re-embedding the anchors. This had included pissing on one of them because earlier in the climb Ginette had told me that frozen urine would really cement anchors in place. Now whether we would survive or not was dependent on the manufacture of the tent. At first the poles held out, buckling in on us but eventually some of them broke up, and the flapping and banging intensified. The rip-stop nylon however refused to rip, even though the broken poles put holes in the fabric. At one point one of the ice axe anchors pulled out and started flying around, crashing again and again into the tent. By sheer luck I managed to grab it, and with every ounce of heaving strength fought it through the quickly unzipped door, and cut it free. With great difficulty we dressed in all our gear, including our boots, in case the tent disintegrated completely, and got back into our sleeping bags. We remained on station propping up the remnants of the aptly named North Face tent. We knew it would be hard to survive if the north wind split us open and the cold and snow came in.

We were obviously both scared, but no panic entered our actions, in fact part of me revelled in the wildness of the experience. I laughed and shouted expletives into the howling, banging, moonlit night like "Fucking amazing" and "Quite incredible, quite incredible." There was a small part of me that cried to be free of this, now, but it was easy to control, the stronger part of me was high on the madness of it all. Patience and watchfulness were the key.

Eventually we dozed fitfully. It was an intense experience that I shared with a man I had grown to respect and like, and we had acted as a team, with me taking the lead, maybe because unconsciously it was me who was expected to deal with a mountain situation like that. The dawn came and we were both bursting for a piss so each took it in turns to pee into an orange powder drink container. The contents were flung out the door. As the morning wore on ten to twenty second lulls in the wind started to appear, and I knew it was just a matter of time now. The banshees departed and we made a huddle inside our wrecked shelter to get a stove going. We packed, dug out our axes and left the tent, now only tethered by three points. It was like a balloon waiting to take off.

We left and I watched Al as he inexpertly took time to sort out his kit. He was not used to this kind of thing and I prayed he would not fuck up on the vertical descents through the rocks. The broad ridge narrowed, steepened, became knife-edged, and beneath our feet the yawning drops beckoned. We were into the really dangerous section now and it all had to go well. Before the steep rocks plunged down out of sight we stopped and I repeated instructions. Al was cool and my optimism was rewarded; he made no mistakes. We abseiled down the worryingly frayed rope for the last time, splayed cramponed feet scraping the vertical granite to a sentry box belay at the top of the Japanese gully. Then three easy rope lengths, and next down the crucial pitches that Finders had led, onto the steep ramp. At the bottom of this Al waited, looking shocked. He had been hit on the shoulder by a small rock, but nothing had been broken and I urged him down. We stumbled down the steep snow cone that lay at the base of the mountain. Harry had taken a four hundred foot fall down this in the early stages and had been lucky not to injure himself. By the time ABC came into sight we were automatons looking for some charity. It felt strange after so long at Camp 1 and 2 to be back in the land of the living.

The next day we packed the chaos that remained into two huge red haul bags we called the 'pigs', and into our seam-splitting rucksacks. We burnt the rubbish, left food, gas and my old stove, and turned to look again at Gangkar Punsum. Was she laughing at us? It was as still as could be at ABC, was it now peaceful up there? I told myself not to be stupid, of course it had to be blowing a gale. We said our private goodbyes to her and what she had meant to us. She would keep her millions of years old virginity a little longer, and I stood there hoping that the next bunch of people would be pure enough of spirit, and love her enough, for her to relent. She liked us enough not to kill any of us, and for that we had to be thankful, but she had rejected us. Nobody came right out and said it but I noticed there were many small references by everyone to 'her', that 'she' was a power, an influence, a mystery to be respected.

We turned and dragged the 'pigs' across the glacier to a chorus of 'Rawhide'. I rode one of them down a steep snow slope, which was fun, but I was so bone tired that in a moment of neglect I lost my temper with JJ, God knows why, I just get like that sometimes when I'm at a low ebb. By the time we got to the main glacier crossing I was wasted and fell progressively further and further behind. I had got used to this kind of physical torture, and I'd known worse. In the past I'd cried on my hands and knees for it to stop, that day I just stumbled on, and there was Harry waiting for me on the other side, who else? No one cared as much about his mates as Harry.

Base Camp's green meadow, stunted bushes, and lakeside prime location was a mental massage and we received a handshake welcome from all the staff, understood there was basically only rice and dhal to eat, and were told the helicopters were expected in three days' time.

CHAPTER 18

Alone with Ginette

ON THE FACE OF IT WE WERE A RELAXED, relieved to be alive bunch, looking forward to our first beers and steaks and the thrill of the helicopter ride back to Paro. But I guess the absence of success, and too long together, gave growth to a mould of discontent. The next morning at the 'stuff in as much as you can' breakfast a discussion took place about fetching some loads that we had left behind on the glacier. We had agreed at ABC that we would all go across with some of the staff and pick it all up in one go. Now the malingerers showed their colours. Lydia suddenly had a cold, not that it was in evidence afterwards, and Monksie argued that it was not necessary for us all to go, and that he would stay behind. I told him exactly what I thought, that it was not fair on those who were prepared to go, and that basically he was just being lazy. We argued about the quantity of stuff to be fetched. Certainly if he was right he had a point; but to decide unilaterally was selfish, and in any case the more of us that went the less of a back breaking job it would be. They stayed, the rest of us went, and I found myself at the back with Ginette.

We just talked and talked and talked. It was so nice. Just sunshine, the glacier and her. She was one of five children. She said she was very fond of her younger brother. He was out of work living in a Housing Association flat, played the drums, and was bit of an artist. She was the only one of her family who had been to university. Her mum had gone back to nursing after twenty nine years, after her father had had a major heart operation. He had been a drugs rep and a year after the op had set up his own business as a management consultant.

It was great to walk with no load in the rucksack for a change. We met Finders at the edge of the moraine leading to the glacier crossing. He had forgotten his goggles and was now dithering about going on. I told him he was crazy to even think about it. The result of going on would be severe headaches, maybe even snow blindness. He reluctantly turned back.

We edged our way across the mess of slag and ice and she, like me, expressed surprise at the fact that some of the others couldn't wait to be away. She loved this place, so beautiful, so peaceful, why should anyone want to leave. It was so precisely what I felt too. As we walked I was looking for a special stone to take home. It was a superstitious thing. I brought one back from every expedition. I found it on the way back, perfectly black and white. Quartz and mica. I wondered whether the issues, the moral questions with Ginette, were just as black and white. I doubted it.

She expressed doubt, misgivings about her relationship with Jules back home. Jules had his own unfathomable problems that the rest of us spent a fair amount of time speculating about. He was a fascinating rebel with bohemian leanings. He rarely got out of bed before midday, spent hours playing his grand piano while his life decayed around him. He was a dentist but hadn't bothered to work for a while, owned a dark Georgian house in Clifton, a couple of properties in one of the worst parts of Bristol that he had just simply forgotten about, and was delightfully absent minded and charming. He'd had a bad accident, I think, and the surgeons had removed a circular piece of bone from his forehead. There was an indentation there that lent character to his rather wild intellectual appearance. We thought the removal of the bone had probably enhanced his third eye powers. He was also a brilliant rock-climber. One day Jules was going to have to face up to life, but not yet awhile.

I cautiously ventured that I thought they seemed to be not entirely happy together. She said it was true, and that it was more on her side than it was on his. I had guessed as much anyway. Jules's relationship with Ginette was one of his props.

I talked about the love of my life, Bente, a Norwegian girl who lived with me for a year and a half, when I was twenty two. I confessed the pain of her leaving, and the sense of betrayal when she had taken off with a friend of mine. How even then I had never stopped loving her and always would. We rambled on about relationships. We smiled and joked, and just like the other times when I found myself alone with her, it seemed so natural. Her voice had a soft, direct intimacy, like we had always been friends and knew it was okay to say anything, discuss anything. It was a game of testing for responses; with neither of us knowing what it was we were looking for or what we wanted. Still, it was easy and fun.

We arrived at the lunch spot, where the abandoned loads were, to find that there were a lot of personal things that had been left behind by Monks and Lydia. It did nothing to endear them to us and there was general moaning about the inequity of this. Even with eight of us the loads were quite heavy. Phuntso the cook, half the size of us, seemed to have a load twice the size of ours but on the way back soon stretched an unassailable lead. Even competitive Harry was not able to keep up with him. Ginette and I stayed behind sunning ourselves on the rocks and dozing. We gave the others half an hour start and then moved back slowly, talking all the while. I described in detail our upbringing; the romantic rented manor house, the doubly romantic servant's quarters of a deserted mansion, the strict father and our adorable mother.

Inevitably, as we knew we would, though it took all day to get to it, we moved on to talking about Monksie. Truth has a habit of pouring out and before I could engineer perfect tact, I said how bad it was, I thought, that within days of parting from Jane he had set off on a deliberate seduction of her. I said how could he love Jane and two minutes later be after someone else.

She replied that she wasn't sure what her own morals were, what was right and wrong, but anyway weren't holiday romances okay? She had in any case heard rumours of Jane, Monksie's girlfriend, playing around on the side, and maybe I was a bit naive. She went on to say there were things she did not like about Steve. She thought he had a big ego. I said I had noticed a distinct change from the happy go lucky, all for one and one for all Steve that I had first known. Now that he had become a super hard, celebrity climber there was a harder edge to him. Although nothing was said, clearly something had happened and I concluded the thing with Steve was over.

Suddenly she said, "…and what sort of girl do you think would suit you Steve?" It was said quietly, eyes averted. Was this just a question from one friend to another? Was it flirtatious? Did she want me to tell her already what I felt? I just laughed light-heartedly and said, "Someone like you Ginette, I think you're wonderful, but you are going to be travelling all round the world all the time. It would never work out." Back in camp I noticed she had moved out of Monksie's tent into Capt. Kathmandu's.

We gathered in the evening for another identical frugal meal, and we were all pretty relaxed until I brought up the subject of who should go out on the first chopper. I said I thought it ought to be Al, Finders and Harry. Al wanted to do some filming in Thimphu, Finders wanted to be part of it, and I said I thought Harry more than anyone deserved it as he had spent huge amounts of time supporting us from Base Camp.

Monksie chipped in that he thought the issue should be up for discussion. At which I retorted that how could he expect to leave his personal belongings on the glacier, leave it to the rest of us to pick them up, and the other loads, and then expect to go out first on the helicopter. To which the others agreed and Steve backed off, actually with good humour. We were still friends, even though the cracks were a little wider, and we enthusiastically got stuck into a good game of cards. That was the funny thing, we were still a good company of friends, but the failure brought out the microscope of bacterial self-examination. We were so close that we could ride the minor back-biting and we knew these tensions were partly a result of that failure. Nevertheless it went on, and we each in our own way made judgments.

The following day we hoped the helicopters would come but they did not. We packed, I listened to some Frank Zappa, we joked and enjoyed the sunshine. I asked people to leave any presents they wanted to give to the staff outside my tent. Later I went for a walk down by the lake. A gentle breeze stirred the water. Gangkar Punsum lorded the scene, clouds and snow plumes pouring from her ridges. It seemed to me some people were busy in the waiting-room impatient for the train to arrive, while others of us stood on the platform waiting for the same train, but still engaged with what was around us. I for one felt a real sadness to be leaving, a melancholy.

At five thirty the next morning Finders, Jeff and I got up and walked for an hour to a small lake in the valley above us to the west. Clouds coiled among the twenty thousand foot peaks that separated us from the remote district of Lunana. Sunrise rays painted them briefly pink. They were moments of the rarest beauty and we all three stood rooted to the spot until the climax had passed.

Back in camp there was more wrangling on the radio. We heard the choppers had left Paro at ten and that it was a forty five minute flight. At twelve we heard that they had returned to Paro as they could not find us. In the morning as we were packing two large ravens came into camp cawing and behaving as though they owned the place. Harry said it was an omen that the helicopters would come today, and there would be two of them. I again allowed anger to spoil my day when it emerged that Monksie and Lydia were the only two not to give presents to the staff. Sure we were all impoverished climbing bums, but much of the clothing had been given to us free, and we were incomparably wealthy compared to our loyal, hardworking staff. I stomped around saying how sick it made me feel. Nobody wanted this tarnished finish to the trip, but there was agreement from everyone that they should have given something. At lunch there were a few pointed remarks, something about how Steve could have at least given his camera away as it wasn't working in any case; a biting comment that clearly hurt.

At 2.15 p.m. the two whirlybirds arrived, all Perspex, noise and wind. There was a general rush towards the landing ground while I stayed back and filmed on Al's Keystone Autoload. One machine took off, hovered for a minute or two and then landed again. I saw Findlay jump out. Al jumped out of the second one, and it too took off and high tailed it down the valley. Harry came over and with a certain contempt said, "Guess who was in them Steve – Monksie and Lydia." It was an unbelievable show of selfishness, and so sad, and there was universal condemnation. We couldn't understand though why the helicopters had only taken one person each. On the squeak box we heard that our friends were being taken to Bumthang, and that the pilots were going to come back and take some more people to Paro. There was general mirth and even jubilation that this might happen, as it would mean that Monksie and Lydia would get stuck in the middle of Bhutan and have to travel back to Thimphu by road. We waited and waited, and then on the radio we discovered that in fact they had been dropped at Tongsa. The helis had come back for us, but never made it due to cloud cover. They had turned round and gone back, picked up Steve and Lyd, and carried on to Paro, where we all imagined the two of them would jump into bed with each other again.

We were not the only ones who felt fed up; the staff were by now voicing their feelings. They said it was clear to them that they were going to be expected to find a way down by the glacier and then down the river valley, thus avoiding going back over the passes. No-one had been down this way, and they were worried about it. I promised to plead on their behalf when I got down to Paro or Thimphu. We had also been told that the leader and the doctor would be the last to be picked up. Such irony.

The next day dawned clear and at 9.15 a.m. we heard the drone of high flying aircraft, but this time although we had lit a fire the two helicopters flew past us and disappeared behind Gangkar Punsum. After what seemed an age they reappeared and came into land. As agreed Al and Finders hopped in, and then the pilot, having taken a suck on his oxygen tank through a tube, climbed out and took photographs of Gangkar Punsum. He dropped off some provisions, undoubtedly for the staff walk out, and with a superior expression that upper notch

Indians master so well, took off again. We waved an enthusiastic goodbye, and waited again. Finally three hours later and Harry and Capt. Kathmandu also lifted off leaving Ginette and I alone again.

To me, then, it seemed as if everything that I had done in my life had brought me to this point. Alone with this attractive woman, who I knew I understood very little, but in whose company I felt so much at home. It seemed that we both knew we were going to be left behind together. We had not wanted to get on board the helicopters.

CHAPTER 19

Waiting

THEY DID NOT COME AGAIN, God knows why. In the evening we sat alone in the mess tent together and the staff entered shyly to serve the rice, yak meat, cabbage and fried potatoes. The nudging and winking was going on out of sight no doubt. We talked about the day's events and went to bed, in my tent.

Ginette went in first, undressed and climbed into her sleeping bag while I stood outside togged out in my down clothing stamping my feet trying to keep warm, telling myself nothing was going to happen. As always I watched for a shooting star in the star-spangled ceiling, but nothing from the universe fell and I made no wishes. When we were both inside she lit a candle. I wish I could remember all the detail of the things we said. We lay facing each other, cocooned in down, and we talked about girlfriends of mine, boyfriends of hers. I felt incredibly aware of her eyes and her closeness, of her page boy style black hair and her long eyelashes. We could manage small glances only, anything longer would have been too much to handle. Eventually that happened and I leant forward and kissed her lightly. How I longed to hold her. All she said with a shy grin was, "Now Steve control yourself."

Like a tortoise I pulled my head back inside my sleeping bag, and nervous now at the thought I might be rejected I asked her what sort of man she wanted. It was table tennis with words; each looking for the right opening, for the correct shot to play. She replied without pause with down turned eyes, "Someone who is kind, gentle, fun, has a sense of adventure, but not an extrovert, yeah that's it Steve."

The words held me in shocked confusion. She must surely know that she was describing me. The candle flickered, she looked so pretty and yet so sad. She said she wanted to have kids, but admitted that at the age of twenty eight it was beginning to feel late. We agreed it would be nice to live in the country to bring up kids. I talked again of my childhood in Oxfordshire, how great it was to explore the overgrown rose gardens sunk deep in the forest, which had taken over when the grand family had fallen on hard times. The grottoes, the monkey puzzle tree, the semi-circular marble seats in the woods, the system of artificial moats, and the island covered in tiny gravestones for the dogs of past packs. I enjoyed the storytelling but all the time we both knew we would come back to relationships. The insecure male in me wanted to find out the extent of the competition. I asked did she fancy Jeff? She replied she did. She thought he was very good looking, but she hastily added she thought he was too fond of his girlfriend Sue for anything to happen with him. It was a reassurance of a sort; the door was still open.

The problem was there were too many men she had relationships with. Jules was not the only one. She told me of another man in the States, but he too seemingly had a girlfriend, and there was Monksie. On so many levels she seemed to have the right qualities for me, but she had too many men to choose from, and chasing her. She had projects to follow in America, Nepal and New Zealand with high altitude medicine, and through the immediate heat of desire I found myself thinking she had not seen the need for an exclusively one to one thing yet. I knew that is what I wanted. I wanted that special relationship that you only have with your own family around you. To hell with all these casual relationships.

We finally blew out the candle and lapsed into silence. God, I wanted her, the time was now. "Please come over here and cuddle me G." A rustling and movement and we were holding each other, stroking each other's hair, cheek to warm cheek, kissing, tongues swirling. Moans and sighs, words pouring out. She doesn't want to hurt me, I'm too nice. I told her how long I've wanted her, she knew, and we admitted many things. We laughed about the fight and me biting her neck. We talked again about Jules and she told me that before we left England she had said to Jules, "What happens Jules if I come back madly in love with Steve?" meaning me. She said she knew she didn't love him, but that if she made love to me then that it would not be for fun, it would be because I wanted love.

I sensed that she would back off from me tomorrow, but just then I could not have been happier, holding her, sleeping next to her, waking up every now and then and kissing occasionally, but I knew she had so many issues to resolve, and the response was friendly only. I realised she needed time.

It had been cloudier that evening and I had the distinct feeling that the weather was slowly breaking. The next morning the Mangde Chu valley was full of cloud, and that was the way the 'copters came. On the squelchy radio we heard that a machine had left Paro at 8.30 a.m. It never arrived. It tried again at midday but again there was too much cloud. By mid afternoon cloud had covered all the nearby ridges and peaks, as well as filling the valley. Our camp seemed to be the only sunny spot.

Battling with the radio took hours of patient and impatient twiddling of knobs, and sometimes getting a contact literally took hours. We now understood why they had sent a radio operator with us. Tobgay used to disappear into his radio tent and you could hear him tapping out Morse before he switched to audible reception. Even then you could only count on being able to hear a varying percentage of what was being shouted into the mike in Thimphu. Sentences had to be short and simple; complicated questions were just not possible. Everything had to be repeated and as the days wore on we felt increasingly powerless and angry with the equipment, with Thimphu and especially with the pilots.

At 3.00 p.m. that day Tobgay finally got through and, thankfully, Monksie was there in Thimphu helping to decipher my voice from the hisses, burps, whines, and crackles that the stone age equipment made. I was told that they might try again the next day, but there was a doubt about it as there was a festival in India and it was thought that the pilots might want to go to it. Thimphu then landed a bombshell. They told me that our expedition equipment might not be flown out and how did I feel about it being brought out later? Most of it was still with us at Base Camp and our agreement with Air India was that it went free as accompanied baggage with the team. If it had to follow on later it would cost us money we did not have. I conveyed this as politely as possible. I also expressed deep concern for the safety of the Bhutanese staff who were expected to trek out on an untried route. All I received to that was crackling ether.

Ginette had retreated into quietitude. She left me to get on with the stuff with Thimphu and read a book most of the day. In the evening we played cards and ate the same boring meal. No mention was made of the previous night and of our words of love and confession. Eventually we went to bed as before but this time there was silence. The light went out and so it started. Did I want to talk? Round and round we went; love, morality, loneliness, Jules, Monksie and the American. I revealed my hurt at hearing her and Monksie making love. She said she hadn't realised she had been hurting me. She said I had the wrong impression of her in any case, and that she was as much at fault as Monksie was. She confessed she had had affairs with married men and that she couldn't be faithful to anyone. I told her of my need to have someone as close to me as my family, and how shallow I thought the temporary relationships were. Unconsciously I was driving her further from me. I realise that now, but at the time I thought my arguments for one-to-one love were absolute truths. She was thinking no doubt that how could I have expected love to be a believable truth when she was involved with Jules, having a fling with a guy in America, and we both knew she had been cheating with Monksie.

Like my first ever crush on a girl there was an aching longing, but she had decided to close and bolt the door to passion. She said, "Steve, let's wait and see how we feel in Bristol. We've had it all between us, except for the other thing. Let's not spoil it. Let me see how it works out with Jules." After all the talk of love the previous night the rejection was painful and confusing. I struggled vainly to find the words to put time in reverse, and go back to the beginning. Somewhere I had stepped over an unseen mark and now her position was polarised. She had decided either I was just another guy after her for sex, or that she couldn't live up to the things I wanted from the relationship. Shame was I wanted it all: love, sex, friendship, fun, intimacy, commitment, the whole damn works.

I just could not understand why this had all gone wrong. She was not some brainless idiot. She was a highly intelligent woman. Hadn't she seen the value of love? Love was maybe too easy with so many men chasing after her all the time. But in fact, underneath, another part of me said she was doing the right thing; that she was right to say no to intimacy if love was ever to get a look in. Maybe she was stronger than me after all. Right then I would have settled for the here and now, for the ton up adrenalin of nakedness and her legs wrapped round my back.

Finally we hugged each other and stayed like that for ages. Next she deliberately tried to make me face up to the reality of life when we got down from the mountain, by asking how I would feel if she slept with Monksie again in Thimphu. It was a painful thought. It was all so confusing. Why was the lovely girl I thought I knew so messed up? And if she was so shallow why hadn't she simply just taken advantage of me for sex as well? She woke up in the night and sat up seeming to me to be talking in her sleep. I caressed her head, her ears, sat up and kissed her, pulled her down, but she just turned away leaving me desolate.

Every day when we woke up the two ravens were there hopping around outside our tent. It seemed like they were asking what had happened in the night, wishing us well, sympathising with our situation. At 9.00 a.m. the next day there was a radio call and I was asked how much all the gear weighed. I said we would weigh it, but I asked for a guarantee that the gear would be taken out first. Displeasure at this over the air-waves but they promised to get back to me at three in the afternoon. No helicopters today, and ironically while the Indian pilots were enjoying their religious festival the weather was perfect. G and I at least had something to do. We were still smiling and friendly. She knew I was just lonely. There was 45 kgs of expedition kit, 184 kgs of personal gear and 218 kgs of film equipment. We read, dozed, had lunch and were stuck to the circumference of camp. We could never go far as there was always a chance of radio contact or helicopters. Lying just to the north of us were the most exciting uninhabited mountains, valleys and glaciers. We had seen this magical place from high on Gangkar Punsum; a string of unvisited peaks plumb on the border with Tibet, all still waiting for a future generation with the right permits and the right attitude.

At tea time she said, "No more deep conversations tonight Steve. I just want to sleep." It was final, dismissive. She was cutting herself off from me. I knew that at the height of last night's agony aunt conversations, I had thrown in her face questions about why she had affairs with married men. I'd asked didn't she realise the damage that resulted. What about the damage she did to other people, I had said. In fact I had really gone too far. At tea I apologised for my behaviour, and she replied there was nothing to be ashamed of. Dinner was boiled potatoes with ground chilli dip and salt, and red rice. Everything was running out; I had run out of my Indian beedi cigarettes, and being an addict was reduced to cannibalising dog ends from the mess tent floor. During dinner in the freezing mess tent we had little to say, each occupied with our own thoughts.

The previous night she had told me Monksie had an 'open' relationship with Jane, and that she was OK about him telling his girlfriend, Jane, about their affair. Yet at the same time she had said she felt it was OK for her to be unfaithful to Jules, provided he didn't find out. She asked me to keep quiet about it. Is love, real love, able to shrug off any infidelity? Is screwing around OK by mutual consent, and would love have the same value? How was it she could screw Monksie when she had openly said there was a lot about him she did not like? Every time my mind accused her of something bad a split second later it had a nasty habit of looking at my own actions. Given half a chance I too would have sinned against my friend Julian. I argued at least I knew she didn't love Jules, whereas she had slept with Monksie knowing he was in a supposedly loving relationship.

In the tent no words were spoken other than "Goodnight." I slept on and off and Ginette talked and moaned in her sleep. It was agony being next to her, and I wished we could start again and get it right. I wished she would change her mind and that we could just sweep the muck under the carpet, but these were vain hopes that lay in the silly thoughts at the edge of my consciousness.

The next morning she got up at six and went for a walk, whilst I separated the gear into 150 kgs loads and read a spy thriller. After lunch I followed her on a walk around the lake that lay below our camp. There was a great gulf between us, a sadness. We sat down at the furthest end of the lake. It was so beautiful there; the sun sparkled on the placid magic lake creating flashing patterns like thousands of fireflies. Gangkar Punsum towered above, her never changing beauty by then taken for granted. Occasionally we could just catch the muted grumble of the radio generator. We sat there unhappy, pretending we were OK. We wandered down the small valley that led towards the Mangde Chu river. The two ravens had followed us croaking their friendly but indecipherable communications. We sat down and from behind I tipped her hat. She smiled at me and we both knew. She left me then and carried on around the lake, and a mist rose up outlining her against the shore. Somehow the magic lake had made us both feel better and we joked easily at tea. That night we talked happily until 10 p.m., slept for three hours and at 3 a.m. in the morning woke up and talked again for another two hours. We were friends again.

The next day arrived and we were told that the helicopters had not come from India, even though the day before Thimphu had given categorical assurances that they would. The problem was that the Bhutanese did not own their own helicopter and had to go cap in hand to the Indian Airforce. Before even asking for a helicopter the need for one had to be cleared through several ministries in Thimphu and then, I think, the Bhutanese army had to put in a request to their opposite number through the Indian Embassy. From there the request had to be passed through various Indian channels and, if the Indians agreed, then the helicopters would have to fly from their base in Bagdogra, and herein lay the real problem. Bagdogra lay a long way from the Bhutan border, on the Indian plains below Darjeeling. We had seen through all the days of waiting that the weather was usually perfect first thing in the morning, but by the time the machines arrived more often than not the cloud had welled up, and the pilots quite naturally turned back for fear of flying into a mountainside. I had urged them to base themselves in Paro to enable an early start, but they refused, apparently insisting on returning each time to their base in Bagdogra. Probably a refuelling issue we thought.

In any case they did not lift off and by now Ginette and I seriously doubted that they would ever come at all. In the morning I walked for several hours to the top of the glacial moraine that hemmed in the magical lake, to get the views of the main glacier, and to be on my own. After lunch she offered to trim my beard and I enjoyed her laughter, the intimate contact, her stroking my face. We lay in the sun. She wore shorts, her legs level with my face and it took all my control not to roll over and start kissing her legs. The frustration was maddening. Another shouting match with the radio at 3 p.m. told us that all the telephone lines with India had been 'down' for the last three days, but that the pilots were absolutely definitely coming for us tomorrow. Harry and Monksie were coming to meet us at Paro it seemed.

I am afraid that another moderately heavy conversation started at tea time, born of frustration. I asked her why would she rather sin with Monksie than have something decent with me? She answered that it was because it was convenient sex with no involvement. But why, why was she so scared of involvement and love? Couldn't she see that it was wrong to be entering into something that could wreck other peoples' lives. It was the answers I wanted, not to attack her. Who the hell was I to take the moral high ground anyway! I wanted her to know that mine was not a clean slate either. I told her I wanted her to know that there had been plenty of occasions when I had slept with women just for the sex, knowing perfectly well that I wanted it to go no further. I listed a few; people we knew, and I confessed that afterwards I had felt degraded, ashamed of myself, because I knew it had been wrong. We retired to sleep in our tent again. I made an attempt to be light hearted saying why was it that here I was, an averagely attractive man, with a few material benefits, and that all I wanted was a good friend and lover, and all I ever got was rejection? I said it with bounce, making a joke, but I was wondering again what it was that had left me without a partner. Why was it that most people achieved the love thing seemingly easily enough, and yet it was always so difficult for me. Why?

I drifted off to sleep. My back had been hurting at the base of my spine all day and I woke up in some pain. Suddenly my feelings of hurt, non-comprehension, frustration and now physical pain all focused at once and I just wanted to hit back. "I wish I had never invited you on this trip. I am so unhappy. This time together should have been fantastic but it's ruined. Why is it, what the hell is wrong with me?" Although not actually crying I think I was sobbing and she rolled over and tried to comfort me. She said she was so sorry she had hurt me. I immediately regretted what I had said and said I was so, so sorry. She started crying. What a mess!

We held onto each other and talked and talked. I told her about my brother's suicide, and the grief and hurt just poured out, and in a moment of weakness I told her I loved her. It was probably a big mistake. The doctor in her came out and she found an expedition heat pad (meant for helping with cases of frostbite) and put it under the base of my spine. In no time it worked wonders. We somehow got back on an even keel and I must have asked her two or three times if she forgave me. Out of this madness of not knowing what to believe, and in another reasonable attempt at humour, I said, "You know G I guess what it boils down to is that you fancied Monksie more than me." She said she was scared of being involved and it was all so intense. Why, what the hell for? All I wanted was a true friend, a stable relationship and to make love.

Of course the helicopters never made it the next day either. After some broken, half understood, half talk on the radio we gathered that one machine only had left Bagdogra, and it had then stopped at Paro. It left there at 9.40 a.m. Too late again. The cloud had moved in and it never arrived. They tried again after lunch and failed. We were incensed that no one would take any notice of what we repeatedly told them. That they *had* to be with us by 8.00 a.m. in the morning or it was too late. Trouble was I could just see the scenario at the Indian Airforce HQ; all stiff upper lip, handle bar moustaches, ridiculous bureaucracy and an inability by anyone to take the initiative to fly really early. More than my job's worth in the most subtle of all Indian ways. We decided that if there was no absolute guarantee at the next day's early morning call that we would start the walk out. The potatoes had now run out and we were basically down to lentils and rice; mind you I liked lentils and rice. The days were so repetitive; 6.30 a.m. bed tea, 7.00 a.m. the sun hit the tent, we got up, went to the toilet, tried the radio, breakfast was at 8.00 a.m., we dried the frost-coated sleeping bags in the sun and by midday the sun was too hot, by 4.00 p.m. it was getting cold, 5.30 p.m. it was just about dark, feet were frozen by 6.30 p.m., dinner, and we were into bed by 7.30 p.m.

We were sentenced for an indeterminate time in the most perfect prison ever invented, where happiness was a kiss away, but unhappiness was the only course. Where there was seemingly no escape and rescue an ever dwindling remote possibility. Still in spite of our situation life was often sweet. We talked endlessly with our Bhutanese friends about their strange society, its legends, its gods and its royal family. I played chess with the Radio Operator, and Ginette tried learning elements of the Tibetan-like language. We read books, took photographs, and listened to music until all the batteries were dead.

At four in the afternoon that day we managed to make contact again to hear that our team was leaving Bhutan tomorrow, and that just Jeff was staying behind. We were told again that maybe there would be a helicopter tomorrow. What a joke. After dinner we went for a walk in the dark up to the small lake some way above camp for something to do. We saw a shooting star and she said she knew what my wish was. I wondered then whether she was like the mountain, just an impossible dream. Up on Gangkar Punsum I had pushed my body and my luck as far as it would go, any further and I believe I would have died. Did I have to try even harder to win Ginette or was it all just a waste of breath? Is success purely a matter of how much total commitment one has? Was my lesson on the mountain that I simply had to try harder, to never give up. I didn't think so; there is a limit for everything.

At 8.00 a.m. the next morning we were told a helicopter was coming but there was more cloud down in the Mangde Chu valley than there had ever been at that time of the morning. We thought they stood no chance of getting through. We told Thimphu we wanted to start walking but they pleaded with us to wait until the midday call. We agreed. We were on the brink now but thought that it was probably snowing or raining heavily down in the valley below. Walking out would have been a miserable ordeal. High winds on Gangkar Punsum were forming massive cloud trails which, blown by the prevailing winds, went straight down the Mangde Chu valley. The chopper left at 9.38 a.m. but never got through. At 12.00 p.m. Thimphu told me that the pilots had at long last agreed to station themselves in Paro for an early morning lift tomorrow. By now it was too late to start walking out, and we felt that with an early start they must get through. Tomorrow, it had to be tomorrow or we really would have to walk.

The next day was a crazy day. We woke to perfect weather and then from 7.00 a.m. onwards we just got a string of contradictory information through the radio. First we managed to raise the Paro airport radio operator who told us that the pilots had not stayed at Paro after all, but we were told that they had left India at 6.40 a.m. and that they were going to come straight to Base Camp. One and a half hours we guessed. We sat and watched and waited, strained our ears and kept looking vainly at our watches. What could possibly have happened we asked each other; bad weather in India? Technical problems? Ran out of fuel? Crashed? Stopped in Paro? Several abortive radio attempts later we finally heard voices through the crackle, and discovered that the pilots had been *expected* to leave India at 6.40 a.m. but in fact hadn't. Well were they coming or not we asked? No-one seemed to know. No-one could find anyone with any authority. I repeatedly and loudly told the operator that he must tell the authorities urgently that if there was no pick-up by 10.30 a.m. we were going to leave. At 10.30 a.m. we were asked to wait until 11.00 a.m. and to make ready, the chopper was on its way. The senior Bhutanese with us, Gopa, wanted to have permission from Thimphu before leaving, so we waited. At 11.00 a.m. we were told it had absolutely definitely left India and was coming straight to us. At 12.30 p.m. it still had not arrived but we were given an ETA of 12.50 p.m. By now we were all sitting next to the radio tent just staring down the valley. At 1.10 p.m. we had given up hope when we heard it coming. Frantic joy and cheering. All our cursing the Indians and kicking stones angrily gave way to a mad rush for the rucksacks and the cook, Phuntso, was off down to the landing area to light the fire, to guide them in. But then the sounds receded and turned to silence.

Of course it had been perfect weather right up to 12.45 p.m. but then cloud had started to well up. Surely though we thought they could make it through. We waited and waited but nothing. I was so apoplectically angry. I was convinced that the pilots ought to be better employed driving rickshaws not helicopters. A whole day had been wasted, if only they had come early we would have been out and now there was no knowing what the weather would be like the next day. We found out at 3.00 p.m. that they had just got lost! The pilots came on the radio at 3.30 p.m. and I described in words of one syllable how to get to Base Camp, and urged them to stay in Paro and to come between 6.00 a.m. and 7.00 a.m. the next morning. I hoped a measure of sarcasm had gone over their heads. Karchung Wangchuck, the main man in Thimphu came on saying 'he was ashamed to speak to me'. I told him it was not his fault, and that whatever happened we would be walking out at 8.00 a.m. the next morning.

Around 4.00 p.m. I spotted a white spot moving slowly across the sky, they another larger black one, and could then make out they were large birds of some sort flying high. As I watched they were joined by more and more until there were no less than twenty eight eagles choosing their thermals carefully. One or two came over camp only a couple of hundred feet above our tilted heads, black tips to their wings. They were moving north east to south west using mountain ridges as spring boards. Gopa told me it was this time of year that they migrated from Lhasa, but I couldn't be sure how he knew this, and I had meant to ask the Chief Justice, the King's uncle, who we had already met in Thimphu, about exactly what they were. He seemed to be the expert in the country. The white one must have been a fledgling I think. We must have watched them for upwards of an hour. The coming of winter was perhaps prompting them to move south. They knew where they were going, that was for sure.

I hoped it would be the last night with G. She was as cold as ever. Like the mountain I had got so far in knowing her and it had been hard and difficult, yet a joy as well, but the final stage was too much for me because of the unrelenting cold wind, or some obstacle that I could not get past. No matter how long I waited a warm spell never arrived. It seemed strangely ironic. I was keener than ever to escape the frustrating tent.

At 7.00 a.m. on 7th November we were told that the chopper had left Paro at 6.50 a.m. The weather was perfect; nothing could stop them this time. So I put on a twenty rupee bet with Tobgay and Gopa on the time of arrival. It got to 8.15 a.m. and we had almost given up hope again when we heard the irrefutable sounds of mankind's engineering. And then we saw it, a small speck in the sky, flying incredibly high for a helicopter. We figured it must have been nineteen or twenty thousand feet. Ecstatic jubilation and we rushed off to the tents totally convinced we were out of there, but no, the fools flew right past us and then incredibly flew right round the back of Gangkar Punsum. We were dumbfounded. They just could not have missed seeing us, and with perfect weather why were they flying so high anyway, and our instructions on how to find us could not have been clearer. We gazed towards Gangkar Punsum convinced that they would come back, but they didn't. So that was it, even the Bhutanese lads were fully into wasting no more time. They packed the remaining tents and burnt and buried the last of the rubbish. We were just going to abandon most of the gear and carry the smallest, lightest tent. I wondered how I would keep away from her in such a small confined space. Visions of being naked with her at the hot springs welled up in my imagination. Meanwhile in the background Tobgay was using all his talent to make frantic last minute calls to Thimphu. Karchung came on the line literally pleading with us to give them one last chance at 12.00 p.m. He said he would send Yeshey Wangchuck, the Bhutanese climber, with the pilots to show them the way.

None of us believed it would come and simply carried on packing the camp, but we were told it had left at 10.30 a.m. At 12.45 p.m. it appeared over the nearby ridge and then made five passes before finally coming in to land. Ginette and I rushed forwards, Yeshey and the co-pilot jumped out. The latter was intent only on taking photos of Gangkar Punsum. Sacks of supplies for the crew were thrown out and we crammed in with three rucksacks and the small tent. The pilots turned up the power, the airframe shook, the noise reached a crescendo, and we lifted ten feet into the air, but then the machine hesitated and we settled back down again. What the hell was wrong this time! The pilots waved and shouted and we realised they were inviting Yeshey to get back on board. Gopa and the others left behind went crazy with joy, and I clicked away as their laughing faces quickly dropped behind. The pilots occasionally sucked oxygen in small amounts direct from tubes attached to bottles. The noise of the engine and the rotors was an offence to nature and I felt somehow embarrassed that we were intruding so heavily on the mountain's peace and quiet. The co-pilot had a very poor map lying on his lap, and took it in turns to fly down the Mangde Chu valley. The vibration was extreme and I could well imagine the nuts, bolts and rivets shaking themselves loose.

All too soon the big mountains disappeared in the rear view mirror and we bucked in thermals over the foothill ridges. Like at a wedding the minutes flew past far too quickly and I wanted to remember every detail. Real excitement makes the mind a piece of mental blotting paper. We flew right over Tongsa's mediaeval fortress, over the intervening mountains and past Punakha Dzong. We could even see people in the fields looking up and we knew that they knew it was us. We were big news in the tiny kingdom; a source of gossip. We were probably a minor shock to the traditional ways of life of the rural Buddhist Bhutanese, and usually it was only the king who would ever use a helicopter, and then probably only to go down from Thimphu to India. The thought of really tasty food and a beer or two became more and more urgent as we wheeled left past Thimphu and on to Paro.

It was over. We had escaped with our changed lives to pick up the pieces. We had returned to argue the toss about who was going to pay for the helicopters, to more pain from love's labours lost, to the quirky society in Thimphu for a few short weeks while we manoeuvred to extract our expedition gear from Base Camp, and we left with tears in our eyes. We had had a taste of fate and been put to many tests, seen a country whose people understood fate, and who believed in their gods and their powers. Whose king would shortly close all the mountains in his realm to the troublesome intrusion of the rabble that Western mountaineers inevitably are.

We did not deserve to stand on top of Gangkar Punsum, for although all but one of us were not there for fame and fortune, we had forgotten the importance of true selfless friendship.

EPILOGUE

After technology and whirly steel had rescued us from the wilderness and our mental trap, we spent a further two weeks in the capital trying to get the Bhutanese to send the helicopters back for our gear. The vast bulk of it had been abandoned when the poor staff left to trek back on their own. After a most subtle game with the authorities a couple of flights were allowed and Jeff flew up as guide and recovered most of the climbing gear. The film kit was simply left behind. There was nothing more we could do, and in any case we were sure Al and Pete would claim on their insurance. Many years later I heard that the following year a train of yaks had been sent up to salvage whatever was worth keeping. I am informed it was sold in India.

At first, on arriving in Thimphu, I had been told that we would not have to pay for any of the helicopter sorties, except that we might possibly have to pay for the flights to pick up the gear. We were provided with a guide and a driver and one bottle of whisky a day at the hotel, and enjoyed being immersed in polite Bhutanese society. However, as the days dragged by the position changed and I was told we would have to pay for all the flights. There was an unseen powerful hand at work behind the scenes and eventually I was summoned to a meeting with the Minister of Tourism at the Tashihhodzong, the main monastery/ fortress in Thimphu. The meeting was scheduled, re-scheduled, post- poned, re-instated and then the timings put back several times. Something was happening behind the scenes.

According to their own Mountaineering Rules and Regulations I was on reasonably solid ground. They had taken the decision to evacuate; it had not been a joint decision. We had merely acquiesced to their decision, albeit quite happily. Nobody had asked us to pay and we had assumed it was a bit of a public service. I think actually that had it been just a couple of flights it probably would have been, however, I am sure behind the scenes Indian Squadron Leaders, Group Captains and Air Vice-Marshalls had probably got hotter and hotter under the collar and this had translated into pressure for payment from the Bhutanese, via the Indian Embassy in Thimphu.

In Thimphu I wore the Bhutanese costume all the time, because I liked it. It was comfortable, I felt smart in it, and my Bhutanese friends really appreciated it. They were forever pulling the pleats straight and getting the cuffs the right length. When I arrived at the Minister's office there was quite a shock, however, that I was not wearing the traditional white scarf as well, and so his personal aide lent me his, and gave me a quick lesson on how to approach the Minister. He showed me how low I should bow, how to offer the scarf before me, how to make sure my knees were covered, and how I was to address him as 'Dasho', meaning lord.

Dasho Letho was a large powerful looking man whose normally expressionless face was occasionally cracked by a twinkling smile. He looked rather lonely in his vast office. He was an exceptional host and we enjoyed tea and mutual compliments as we slowly eased into the difficulties. Jigme Tshultim was there and where normally everyone around him quaked with fear, the boot was on the other foot and he appeared exceptionally nervous; no doubt the consequences if he was seen to have messed up were worse than I could imagine.

I calmly went over our position and said I regretted that I had been unavailable to discuss the use of helicopters, as I had been up on the mountain, but that in any case if we had thought for one moment we would have to pay we would have walked out from Base Camp, as the staff had done.

Dasho Letho listened politely and, without recourse to heavy argument, a compromise was easily reached, and I agreed to pay two thousand two hundred and forty dollars towards the costs. I did hint that there was a slim chance I could claim on our insurance but at that stage anyway no-one had any idea how much the flights were going to cost. The Ministry even finally threw a cocktail party in our honour, and we left Bhutan with great sadness, but thinking that was the end of the helicopter problem.

However, the following spring an invoice arrived on my doorstep for twenty five thousand dollars along with a schedule of the flights. Luckily our insurers agreed to pay up to a maximum of ten thousand dollars. When I examined the flights schedule closely I realised that many of the flights related to the evacuation of the film crew, who were on a separate permit to the main expedition, and after taking off their flights I was within striking distance of the insurance money I had to play with. In the summer of that year, after a trek through Zanskar, and an ascent of Stok Kangri in Ladakh, I headed down to Delhi to visit the Bhutanese embassy there. I breezed in and persuaded the officials to let me try to phone the Ministry of Tourism. I tried for three consecutive days to get through without success, (Indian telephone lines in those days were notoriously bad) and so then got on a train to Calcutta where I tried again from the Bhutanese Customs office, where I had friends. Eventually I managed to speak to Jigme Tshultim who agreed to let me back in to discuss the problem in person.

Back in the capital two English aid workers, whom I had made friends with after the expedition, gave me space on their floor and with a certain degree of anxiety I went to a meeting with Jigme. I argued my case and said I also did not think I should pay for the flights when the Indians had gone off to fly around Gangkar Punsum. There was a shocked response from Jigme who told me that the Indian Airforce had officially requested permission, before the rescue mission had started, to make photographic reconnaissance flights around Gangkar Punsum. Apparently the Bhutan authorities had refused permission and now were livid that they had clearly been ignored. I was able to show from my diary, and the flight schedules, the exact flights in question. I went on to argue that there were certain other flights where the Indian pilots were clearly at fault for not picking us up and this then fell on sympathetic ears. After deducting these flights, the blatant reconnaissance, and the film crew's lifts, we arrived at the surprising total of ten thousand dollars. Jigme agreed to this sum and I promised to send the money by return from England. This time I obtained a letter that this would constitute full and final payment. The film company, I am afraid, never paid their share of the bill and I think the Bhutanese realised that it was futile even chasing them for it.

I did also have an ulterior motive for making such an effort to get back into Bhutan. Back in England a climbing friend, Steve Bell, and myself had sworn solemnly that we would start a trekking company. I therefore used the spare time in Thimphu obtaining detailed descriptions of all the known trekking routes in their beautiful mountains. I had by then discovered that Maggie Payne did not have a monopoly on dealing with British group travel to Bhutan. Starting from two attic offices Steve and I turned Himalayan Kingdoms Ltd. into a well-respected company. In 1993 we became the first British company to guide paying clients to the summit of Everest. In fact by achieving sixteen people on the summit, including my partner Steve Bell, the expedition became the most successful British Everest expedition there has ever been.

One of those to summit Everest with our expedition in 1993 was Ginette. She signed on as a paying client and walked hand in hand to the summit with Gary Pfisterer, another client. Ginette had finally found her true love, but there was much pain in the process. Gary divorced his wife, and they were married in America in 1997. She was the second British woman to summit the highest mountain in the world, and shortly after this became the second British woman to summit the seven continental summits. She was narrowly pipped to the post on both occasions by Rebecca Stephens. Ginette and Gary then set out in pursuit of climbing all the fourteen eight thousand metre peaks in the world. In May 1998 she became the first woman ever to climb the third highest peak, Kangchenjunga. Early the next year she became the first British woman to climb the fifth highest, Makalu. She had five of the eight thousanders to her credit, when we heard news that she had been swept away in an avalanche whilst attempting Dhaulagiri in Nepal. Gary had been yards behind her when it happened and could do nothing but watch. Not long afterwards she appeared in one of those dreams that was more like reality than it was a dream, and in floods of tears said she knew that when they had been on the summit of Everest it would all end in pain and suffering.

We had remained good friends after Bhutan, even though after we were evacuated I became insanely jealous in Thimphu when she had a fling with one of the Bhutanese guides. On returning to Bristol her relationship with Julian finished and we spent some time together but somehow there was no joy, just a buried sadness and we abandoned our Base Camp ideas of love on the rebound. In later years she became godmother to my eldest daughter, Katie, to whom she always wrote long letters whenever she was off on an expedition, and bought her imaginative presents.

Strangely enough it was the women from our team who were drawn to Everest, not the men, and in 1988 Lydia became the first woman to climb Everest, solo, without oxygen, though nobody believed her at the time. She started with an Australian expedition but left them in the end and joined another team, but did not take a camera to the summit. Her estranged Australian expedition members concluded that she could not have made the summit, after they had pieced together the 'facts' of her ascent and accused her of lying. To make matters worse Lydia, on returning to Kathmandu, at first claimed the ascent but then realising that she might be heavily fined, and banned from Nepal, for not having a valid permit by switching teams, changed her story and claimed not to have been to the summit. It was not until years later that a reporter from the *Financial Times* interviewed climbers who had seen her on the summit day, and he pieced together compelling evidence that she certainly could have made the summit. I believe her, and it is rather a fine coincidence that she remains the only New Zealander to have climbed Everest without oxygen, and that Ed Hillary had been in Thimphu when we started out for Gangkar Punsum.

Bhutan changed my life utterly. In 1988 Himalayan Kingdoms started running treks there and on the second trek to the Dagala Mountains, just south of Thimphu, I met my wife Seraphina. She came as a client on the trek and though nothing happened and I behaved in an entirely professional manner, I did find her attractive and we dated a little back in England. The trouble was she was seemingly immersed in a career as a stockbroker, lived in London, was the eldest daughter of an earl, and I just felt it was never going to work out. I decided that there was no point in pursuing a long distance relationship and we stopped seeing each other. Then six months later I was putting together a trip to climb Stok Kangri again, this time with my sister and one of the Gangkar Punsum Support Trekkers, his wife, and another lady, and so I rang Seraphina up and asked if she wanted to come too. As it turned out we were the only two who managed the 20,082ft/6,121 metres summit, where we dared for the first time to hug each other. At the end of the climb we all flew down from Leh to stay on a houseboat in Kashmir, and Seraphina and I sat next to each other on the flight. Flying right past Nun Kun I was able to proudly point out the route Richard and I had taken to the summit. There was now undeniably a certain something between us and in Srinagar airport, waiting for the flight to Delhi, she fell asleep on my shoulder. We were married less than a year later in Odiham on 31st March 1990.

ACKNOWLEDGEMENTS

So many people have helped me with this book, and there are so many others who have been key players in the expeditions themselves. There are all the mates who climbed with me and shared these times, the support trekkers for Bhutan, the sponsors, patrons, and friends who donated time and money. Many others too like the Sherpa friends without whose hard work we would have got nowhere. This list is just a few of those people I would like to thank, and if I have missed anyone it is not for lack of trying to think of all those who deserve my gratitude.

My wife, Seraphina
My mother and father
Lorna and Dick Broomhead
Peter Goodwin
Prof. Matt Peacock
Jon Barton
Dr. Henry Osmaston *(deceased)*
Dr. John Crook *(deceased)*
Tan McKay
Col. Penjor Ongdi
Alok and Renee Chandola
Wangchuk Kalon
Elizabeth Hawley
Sir Chris Bonington
Gary Pfisterer
Tashi Tenzing
Doug Scott
Phunchok Dawa
Jane Wilding
Rob Jackman *(deceased)*